BARBIE®

Written by

GRETA GERWIG
&
NOAH BAUMBACH

faber

First published in 2023
by Faber & Faber Limited
The Bindery, 51 Hatton Garden
London EC1N 8HN

First published in the USA in 2023

Typeset by Faber & Faber Limited
Printed and bound in Canada

A CIP record for this book
is available from the British Library

ISBN 978-0-571-39016-8
ISBN 978-0-571-39013-7

Contents

BARBIE

Introduction

The journey of *Barbie* has been unlikely from the beginning and, in the end, all the more joyful for it.

In 2019, Margot Robbie approached us about writing the script, and one of us (Noah) was deeply unsure about the whole endeavor. BARBIE?! REALLY?! But another one of us (Greta) had a feeling that the whole concept was so strange and so complex that it could potentially be interesting. This combination of curiosity and doubt turned out to be excellent ingredients for what became the most fun writing experience of our careers.

When we first started tinkering, building a few moments here, a few characters there, it was slow going. It was the pandemic. It was difficult to imagine making movies again and the beautiful communal experience of moviegoing felt like a thing of the past. We wanted to write something that would conjure up the lost world we loved. But also, something that reflected the madness of the reality we all found ourselves in. Ultimately, after many digressions, we thought: If no one is ever going to see this movie, let's go for broke.

We really started making each other laugh. We talked about it all the time. "How does Barbie get into her car?" "What would Ken make of our world?" On walks, at dinner, making coffee. It became a way to entertain each other, to organize our minds, to give each other hope. Suddenly it was the thing that gave our lives shape. The script became our grown-up way of playing with dolls and was also a portal into a future world where we were all once again part of the community of moviegoing, laughing and crying and dancing together.

When it was finished, we were both in love with it. It made us happy just that a piece of writing like this existed. We were proud of it, but doubtful that anyone would be mad enough to make it.

And then, miracle of miracles, we gave it to our collaborators (Tom, Margot, David) and after that our decision-makers (Mattel and Warner Bros.) and although there were plenty of questions, ("Does a Mattel executive have to get shot on page 102?"), there was a real enthusiasm to make the movie.

We took every "yes" we got and ran. We drove it like we stole it. We are so grateful that it is in the world.

Greta Gerwig & Noah Baumbach, 2023

Cast and Crew

Cast

Crew

Directed by
GRETA GERWIG

Written by
GRETA GERWIG & NOAH BAUMBACH

Based on 'BARBIE' by Mattel

Produced by
DAVID HEYMAN, p.g.a.
MARGOT ROBBIE, p.g.a.
TOM ACKERLEY, p.g.a.
ROBBIE BRENNER, p.g.a.

Executive Producers
GRETA GERWIG
NOAH BAUMBACH
YNON KREIZ
RICHARD DICKSON
MICHAEL SHARP
JOSEY McNAMARA
COURTENAY VALENTI
TOBY EMMERICH
CATE ADAMS

Director of Photography
RODRIGO PRIETO, ASC, AMC

Production Designer
SARAH GREENWOOD

Set Decorator
KATIE SPENCER

Edited by
NICK HOUY, ACE

Music Supervisor
GEORGE DRAKOULIAS

Music by
MARK RONSON
ANDREW WYATT

Visual Effects Supervisor
GLEN PRATT
FRANÇOIS DUMOULIN
VIKTOR MULLER

Special Effects Supervisor
MARK HOLT

Costume Designer
JACQUELINE DURRAN

Casting by
ALLISON JONES
LUCY BEVAN

Hair & Makeup Designer
IVANA PRIMORAC

Production Sound Mixer
NINA RICE AMPS

Sound Designers / Supervising Sound Editors
AI-LING LEE
DAN KENYON

Re-Recording Mixers
KEVIN O'CONNELL
AI-LING LEE

Barbie

Gerwig/Baumbach

EXT. A DESERT-LIKE-LANDSCAPE. DAY

Like Kubrick's 2001, but with little girls, not apes. And
with baby dolls, not sticks and stuff.

>   HELEN MIRREN (V.O.)
>   Since the beginning of time, since
>   the first little girl ever existed,
>   there have been dolls.

These little girls rock their baby dolls, they burp them,
they cuddle them: <u>They pretend to be Moms</u>.

>   HELEN MIRREN (V.O.)
>   But the dolls were always and
>   forever *baby dolls*. The girls who
>   played with them could only ever
>   play at being MOTHERS. Which can be
>   fun, at least for a while anyway...
>   Ask your mother.
>   (pause)
>   This continued, until...

One of the girls looks UP.

Something has appeared in their midst. Something NEW.
It's a GIANT BARBIE DOLL - BARBIE MARGOT, the 1950s Barbie,
with her black and white swimsuit and lipstick.

The girls react with awe.

They're stirred up and excited by this Barbie Margot not
unlike the apes in that Kubrick masterpiece.

They try to touch her, and one little girl starts smashing her baby doll against the ground until it breaks into pieces. She lets out a child's howl!

One by one the little girls follow suit: whooping, screaming, throwing their baby dolls away in fits of joyful anger.

A final little girl throws *her* baby doll up in the air, and it is spinning, spinning - with a match cut to:

INT. WHITE SPACE

Barbie stands in a empty space of the soon-to-be formed Barbie Land - it's a void, a limbo - but clearly <u>in</u> a film studio. The World of Barbie is a Technicolor Soundstage.

> HELEN MIRREN (V.O.)
> Yes Barbie changed everything! Then she changed it all again!

We go through all the changes to Barbie Margot, as she moves through the decades.

> HELEN MIRREN (V.O.)
> All of these women are Barbie, and Barbie is all of these women. She might have started out as just a lady in a bathing suit, but she became so much more.

We see a row of Barbies. As we move back we see that "Barbie" is a EVERY different kind of woman -- every profession, every ethnicity, every body shape, every different ability and every gift. As we pan by each one, we hear:

> HELEN MIRREN (V.O.)
> She has her own money, her own house, her own car, her own career. Because Barbie can be anything, women can be anything.

We see a Map with Barbie Land on it and a long red arrow is drawn across a split screen to the Real World.

>   HELEN MIRREN (V.O.)
>   (triumphantly)
>   And this has been reflected back
>   onto the little girls of today in
>   the Real World.

Girls playing with the different dolls. The girls all _mirror what their Barbie is._ So the doctor is the doctor, the ballerina is the ballerina, etc.

>   HELEN MIRREN (V.O.)
>   Girls can grow into women who can
>   achieve everything and anything
>   they set their mind to.

Finally, we see a vast sea of Barbies. All in different outfits, different hairstyles, adding new friends, speaking different languages. And now Barbie's world gets continually multi-faceted and wide-ranging and diverse and interesting.

>   HELEN MIRREN (V.O.)
>   (triumphantly)
>   Thanks to Barbie all problems of
>   feminism and equal rights have been
>   solved!
>   (with a knowing smirk)
>   ... at least that's what the
>   Barbies think.

We float above the Barbies into the clouds, then we descend to earth, to see, just below the clouds and above land, the heart-shaped BARBIE LAND.

>   HELEN MIRREN (V.O.)
>   After all they're living in Barbie
>   Land. Who am I to burst their
>   bubble? And here is one of those
>   Barbies now, living her best day
>   every day.

INT. BARBIE DREAMHOUSE. BEDROOM. DAY

Barbie Margot wakes up in her pink Dreamhouse. Everything is perfect. Of course. This whole sequence is like a movie-musical of the best life ever.

There are no walls just like the toy so Barbie Margot can wave across to another Barbie waking up in her Dreamhouse next door.

In every OTHER Dreamhouse, all the Barbies are having *their* perfect morning. It's a Barbie Ballet.

INT. BARBIE DREAMHOUSE. BATHROOM. DAY

Barbie Margot steps out of her heels, revealing her permanently arched feet.

Barbie Margot stands under the shower head, but nothing comes out, she turns her head this way and that, as if there *is* water but there is nothing. Her hair looks amazing anyway.

She opens an AMAZING closet and then magically steps out with a new, perfect outfit!

INT. BARBIE DREAMHOUSE. SLIDE. DAY

Barbie takes her slide down to the pool. Because she can!

INT. BARBIE DREAMHOUSE. KITCHEN. DAY

She eats a nothing breakfast, drinks a big glass of nothing.

EXT. BARBIE DREAMHOUSE. DAY

Barbie Margot stands at the top floor of her house, waves to her friends and then improbably sails through the air and lands in the driver's seat of her car.

>   HELEN MIRREN (V.O.)
>   When you're playing with Barbies
>   nobody bothers to walk them down
>   the stairs and out the door etc...
>   you just pick them up and put them
>   where you want them to go -- You
>   use your imagination!

Behind her, Barbie Alexandra ALSO sails through the air and lands in HER dream car.

Barbie Margot drives and waves at Skipper, in this thing:

Midge appears in Skipper's yard, aggressively waving at Barbie Margot:

>   HELEN MIRREN (V.O.)
>   (butting in)
>   Midge was Barbie's pregnant friend.
>   Oh let's not show Midge actually...
>   she was discontinued by Mattel
>   because a pregnant doll is just too
>   weird. Anyway... Barbie has another
>   BIG day ahead of her.

EXT. BARBIE LAND. DAY

Barbie Margot waves happily, sometimes with both hands, to other Barbies as her car silently drives itself through a bustling town. It's like Richard Scarry's Busy Town for Barbie. It's a wonder of color and shape. The houses are all see-through, like the toys, it's a Noah's Ark of doll-tastic magic.

It's also completely run by women. They hold every kind of job. Barbie Margot waves to a Barbie mail carrier, and an all Barbie construction crew. There is the occasional Ken, but mostly it's Barbie.

Barbie Margot drives past the Barbie White House which is, of course, pink.

INT. BARBIE OVAL OFFICE. LIGHT PINK HOUSE. DAY

Barbie Issa Rae, president (maybe in a ball gown?!) signs a bill into law, surrounded by Barbie Congresswomen. Barbie Margot stands with the press, proud.

                    BARBIE ISSA
          Everybody - turn to the Barbie next
          to you, tell her how much you love
          her. Compliment her! Reporter
          Barbie, you can ask me any question
          you want.

                    BARBIE RITU
          How come you're so amazing?

                    BARBIE ISSA
               (giggling)
          No comment! No seriously, no
          comment.

Barbie Issa looks to the Barbies around her:

                    BARBIE ISSA
          I love you guys!

Hugs, sweetness, support. It is REALLY great here.

INT. NOBEL PRIZE THEATRE. DAY.

A big ceremony, very official, proper. A Barbie Dignitary (in
another flouncy ballgown) presides:

                    BARBIE DIGNITARY
          The Nobel Prize in Journalism goes
          to "BARBIE!"

It's Reporter Barbie! Woohoo! Barbie Margot leaps to her
feet, deeply proud.

                    BARBIE RITU
          I worked very hard, so... I deserve
          it!

                    BARBIE DIGNITARY
          The Nobel Prize in Literature goes
          to "BARBIE!"

It's Barbie Alexandra Shipp! Barbie Margot claps and hoots
from the audience. She's so proud of her friends.

                    BARBIE ANNOUNCER
               (bestowing the prize)
          You're the voice of a generation.

                    BARBIE ALEXANDRA
               (no false modesty!)
          I know.

INT. SUPREME COURT. DAY

Barbie Sharon argues a case passionately in front of the
Supreme Court, all Barbies.

>   BARBIE SHARON
>   Only Barbies are Barbies, and we
>   would argue that corporations have
>   no "free speech" rights to begin
>   with, so any claim on their part to
>   be exercising a right is just their
>   attempt to turn our democracy into
>   a plutocracy!

The Gallery erupts into rapturous applause. Some Kens are
there for support.

>   BARBIE SHARON
>   This makes me emotional! And I'm
>   expressing it. I have no difficulty
>   holding both logic and feeling at
>   the same time. It does not diminish
>   my powers, it expands them.

The Chief Justice Barbie hits her gavel, but she can't help
but smile. Barbie Margot is there, always cheering on, always
the supporter.

EXT. BARBIE LAND. DAY.

Barbie Margot drives past the BAX airport and an airplane
passes overhead, we move up, and the female pilot waves down -

>   BARBIE PILOT
>   Hi Barbie!

- the airplane wipes and we keep moving up to find:

EXT. SPACE. DAY

Astronaut Barbie floats around in space. High fives with
another Astronaut Barbie. Wave down to Barbie Margot, too!

>   BARBIE ASTRONAUTS
>   (in unison)
>   Hi Barbie!

EXT./INT. BARBIE CAR.

Barbie Margot waves up at the astronauts.

>   BARBIE MARGOT
>   Yay space!

Finally she passes and salutes **Barbie Mt. Rushmore.**

Remember this!

EXT. BARBIE LAND. BEACH. DAY

Barbie Margot drives up & hits the beach. This is semi-epic, almost somber in it's initial grandeur.

Ken Ryan Gosling holds a surf board and stands atop of a dune. He's waiting for his Barbie, Barbie Margot.

>   HELEN MIRREN (V.O.)
>   Barbie has a great day every day.
>   But Ken only has a great day if
>   Barbie looks at him.

>   KEN RYAN GOSLING
>   (courageous)
>   Hi Barbie!

Barbie Margot turns and smiles.

>   BARBIE MARGOT
>   Hi Ken!

All the Barbies we just saw are now at the beach - they are *all everything*. Barbie Margot says Hi to Barbies and Ken - or, rather, the Multiplicity of Kens!

>   KEN SIMU
>   (to Ken Ryan Gosling)
>   Hi Ken.

Ken Ryan Gosling groans, waving his hand in dismissal.

>   BARBIE HARI
>   Hi Ken!

>   KEN NCUTI
>   Hi Barbie!

>   BARBIE EMMA
>   Hi Ken!

>   KEN KINGSLEY
>   Hi Barbie!

>   BARBIE ALEXANDRA
>   Hi Ken!

>   BARBIE SHARON
>   Hi Ken!

                   KEN SCOTT
Hi Barbie!

                  KEN KINGSLEY
Hi Ken! I got us both ice creams!

                KEN RYAN GOSLING
Cool.

                  BARBIE ANA
Hi Ken!

Everyone says "Hi Barbie" and "Hi Ken" over and over to each other. Way out in the sea, a few Mermaid Barbies emerge:

                BARBIE MERMAID
Hi Barbies!

               ALL BARBIES AND KENS
Hi Barbie!
        (she disappears beneath
         the waves)
Bye Barbie!

                  ALLAN
Hi Barbie!

                BARBIE MARGOT
Hi Allan!

And there's Allan in his striped shirt. Everything stops.

               HELLEN MIRREN (V.O.)
There are no multiples of Allan.
He's just Allan.

                  ALLAN
I'm still confused about that?

On shore, Ken Ryan Gosling comes sprinting down the sand.

                    KEN RYAN GOSLING
          HI BARBIE!

                    BARBIE MARGOT
          Hi Ken!

                    KEN RYAN GOSLING
          Hey Barbie! Check me out!

Ken Ryan Gosling, who seems to only exist when Barbie is
paying attention to him, runs into the surf, like INTO it,
and flies backward, head over heels, into the air with his
surfboard and...lands HARD.

                    ALLAN
               (Hecuba at Troy)
          KEN! NO!

Barbie Margot and her other Barbie friends jump up and
swiftly coordinate a rescue mission, while the other Kens
stand around helplessly. Ken Kingsley protects his ice
creams.

                    BARBIE MARGOT
               (concerned)
          Ken?

                    KEN RYAN GOSLING
          Oh Hi Barbie... How much of that
          did you see?

                    BARBIE MARGOT
          We saw the whole thing!

                    BARBIE ANA
          Let's get you up on your feet.

Barbie Margot and Barbie Ana lift Ken up.

                    KEN RYAN GOSLING
          Wow you are so strong!

Meanwhile, Ken Simu laughs derisively:

                    KEN SIMU
          Looks like this beach was a little
          too much beach for you, Ken.

                    KEN RYAN GOSLING
          If I wasn't severely injured I'd
          beach you off right now, Ken.

                    KEN SIMU
          Oh, I'll beach-off with you any
          day, Ken!

                    KEN RYAN GOSLING
          You're on, Ken! Let's beach-off!

                    KEN KINGSLEY
               (on Ken Ryan's side)
          Anyone who wants to beach him off
          has to beach me off first.

                    KEN SIMU
          I will beach both of you off at the
          same time!

                    KEN RYAN GOSLING
               (getting upset)
          You don't even know how to beach
          your SELF off how are you going to
          beach all of us off??

                    KEN SIMU
          Why are you getting emotional?!

                    BARBIE MARGOT
          Come on, Kens, nobody is going to
          beach anyone off!

Ken Simu backs off as Ken Ryan collapses into Barbie Margot.

An ambulance pulls up, and FOLDS OUT INTO A HOSPITAL ROOM.

Ken Ryan is put on a stretcher and hurried across the beach.

                    KEN RYAN GOSLING
          Barbie, stay with me!

EXT. / INT. AMBULANCE / HOSPITAL. MOMENTS LATER.

Barbie Alexandra now in her "Doctor" outfit, tends to a small
scratch, while Barbie Hari, also in her "Doctor" outfit,
looks at the results of some x-rays. Barbie Margot stands by.

                    BARBIE HARI
          Not even broken, you'll be just
          fine.

                    KEN RYAN GOSLING
          Shredding waves is much more
          dangerous than people know.

                    BARBIE MARGOT
          You're very brave, Ken.

                    KEN RYAN GOSLING
          Thanks, Barbie. Because you know
          actually my job isn't surfer.

                    BARBIE MARGOT
          I know.

                    KEN RYAN GOSLING
          It's not even lifeguard, which is a
          common misconception.

          BARBIE ALEXANDRA   KEN RYAN GOSLING
     Very common.   Because my job is actually
                                   just, you know, Beach.

                    BARBIE HARI
          And what a good job you do at
          Beach.

                    BARBIE ALEXANDRA
          You should heal up in no time.
          Actually by the time I finished
          that sentence, you healed.

                    KEN RYAN GOSLING
          Fantastic!

He leaps off the table and does an "action man" pose. Then:

                    KEN RYAN GOSLING
          Hey, Barbie - Can I come over
          later?

Barbie Margot and Barbie Alexandra share a look.

                    BARBIE MARGOT
      Yeah, OK. I don't have anything big
      planned, just a giant blow-out
      party with all the Barbies, with
      planned choreography and a bespoke
      song. But you can stop by, sure.

                  KEN RYAN GOSLING
        (with obvious admiration)
    Cool.

EXT. / INT. BARBIE MARGOT'S DREAMHOUSE & STREET. NIGHT.

Barbie Margot has a big block party with all her Barbie
friends, plus Allan and Midge (whom we stay away from!)

DJ BARBIE turns up a song (which is the **AMAZING ORIGINAL HIT
SONG FOR THIS MOVIE**) and there is a GIANT gorgeous musical
number, starring the Barbies! With Kens as dancing
decoration! It's fun and sweeping and funny and a real toe-
tapper all around.

Ken Simu joins Barbie Margot for part of the dance, stoking
Ken Ryan Gosling's ire, who is held back, in a dancing way,
by Ken Kingsley.

Ken Ryan Gosling jumps up and tries to breakdance badly. Ken
Kingsley joins in for moral support..

                  KEN SIMU
      Hey Barbie! Check me out!

Ken Simu does a flip on the dance floor. Ken Ryan Gosling is
enraged. Barbie Margot turns and dances with her friends whom
she'd much rather be dancing with anyway. This leaves the
Kens all dancing together, which is just obviously funny.

Shouting over the music and dancing, Barbie Margot and
friends appreciate how terrific everything is:

                  BARBIE ALEXANDRA
        (while dancing)
    This is a real rager, Barbie!

                  BARBIE MARGOT
        (also dancing)
    THANKS BARBIE! Gosh this night is
    just perfect!

                  BARBIE SHARON
    It's perfectly perfect!

                  BARBIE EMMA
    You look so beautiful Barbie!

> BARBIE MARGOT
> Thank you Barbie! I *FEEL* so
> beautiful!

> BARBIE SHARON
> So do I!

> BARBIE HARI
> This is the best day ever!

Dancing and shouting and so happy it almost hurts:

> BARBIE MARGOT
> It IS the best day ever! And so is
> yesterday and so is tomorrow and so
> is the day after tomorrow and even
> Wednesdays and every day from now
> until FOREVER!

Suddenly, as the flip side of the coin of this thought:

> BARBIE MARGOT
> (still shouting)
> Do you ever think about dying?!

Literal record scratch and everything is quiet. All the
Barbies and Kens look at her. She's broken the movie.

> BARBIE MARGOT
> (to herself)
> I don't know why I just said that?
> (to everyone else)
> I'm just dying to DANCE!

There is panic in Barbie Margot's eyes as she starts
maniacally dancing, doing about eight different dance moves
from over the decades, starting with the Twist, going through
disco, punk, break dancing, etc.

The music picks back up, and she is relieved, although
troubled by what just happened. She shakes it off, and
continues to party. Maybe there is nothing wrong!

LATER THAT EVENING...

After their fun party, Barbie Margot and Ken Ryan Gosling
stand in the moonlight. Ken leans forward for a goodnight
kiss. He gets part of the way there and then pulls back.

> KEN RYAN GOSLING
> (re: the "kiss")
> Wow.

                    BARBIE MARGOT
                 (smiling sweetly)
            You can go now.

                    KEN RYAN GOSLING
            I was thinking that maybe I could,
            you know, stay over tonight?

                    BARBIE MARGOT
            Why?

                    KEN RYAN GOSLING
            'Cause we're girlfriend boyfriend.

                    BARBIE MARGOT
            To do what?

                    KEN RYAN GOSLING
            To... I'm not actually sure...

                    BARBIE MARGOT
            But I don't want you here.

She's smiling her gorgeous smile. Not mean, just truthful.

                    KEN RYAN GOSLING
                 (bummed)
            Ok.
                 (pause)
            Is it Ken?

                    BARBIE MARGOT
            No, Ken is just a good friend.
                 (as if it's comforting:)
            And after all, this is MY
            Dreamhouse. It's *Barbie's*
            Dreamhouse. Not Ken's Dreamhouse.
            Right?

                    KEN RYAN GOSLING
                 (chastened)
            Right as always.

                    BARBIE MARGOT
            And: It's girl's night!

We cut to the other side of them to reveal that all of Barbie
Margot's friends are there, watching it all unfold.

                    BARBIE EMMA (O.S.)
            Come on, Barbie, slumber party!

                    BARBIE HARI
            Come on! The president is here!

                        BARBIE ISSA
          I am. You're welcome!

                     KEN RYAN GOSLING
          Every night is girl's night.

                        BARBIE MARGOT
          Every night! Forever!

                     KEN RYAN GOSLING
                 (nodding)
          Every night.

                        BARBIE MARGOT
          Forever and ever! Goodnight!

She runs back to her friends. They scream and are THRILLED.
Phew, Ken was a LOT!

                     KEN RYAN GOSLING
                 (acting out the fantasy)
          I love you too. But I can't... I
          gotta go.

And then he leaves, thank goodness. She likes Ken, but she
needs her space!

INT. BARBIE DREAMHOUSE, BEDROOM. NIGHT. LATER.

Barbie Margot tucks herself into bed:

                        BARBIE MARGOT
                 (to her Barbie neighbors)
          Goodnight Barbies! I'm definitely
          not thinking about death any more!

Her eyes fly open - she IS THOUGH.

INT. BARBIE DREAMHOUSE, BEDROOM. MORNING.

MORNING! Barbie opens her eyes, ready for an amazing day. But
something is off, she can feel it - she feels groggy, her
eyes don't want to open. She stretches, stiff from sleeping.

She makes a face, cups her hands and smells her breath. YUCK!

INT. BARBIE DREAMHOUSE, BATHROOM. DAY

She brushes her teeth with nothing, but the gesture makes a
difference.

Same shower situation, but suddenly Barbie YELPS and leaps
out of the way of the non-water.

                        BARBIE
            What the--

How was the water that isn't even there COLD?! She adjusts
the knobs and then steps back under the non-water. Better.

KITCHEN

Same breakfast situation, but the plastic waffle is burnt -
how is that even possible? She pours milk into a glass (which
is nothing) and drinks. Spits it out. Looks at the container.

                        BARBIE
            Expired?!

Barbie Margot turns and sees (because remember there are no
walls) another Barbie at her breakfast table, who smiles and
waves. Barbie Margot tries to muscle through it - she's going
to try to smile her way out of this, darn it!

But what is this new feeling? Is it... shame?

EXT. BARBIE DREAMHOUSE. DAY

Barbie Margot stands at the edge of the roof, waiting to be
flown into her car, and she leans into the air and...

FALLS. Just belly flops into the air.

She pops up out from behind her car, trying to save face,
waving.

                    BARBIE MARGOT
                    (to nobody)
            I'm fine! A-ok!

People look at her curiously. What is wrong with her?

EXT. BARBIE LAND. BEACH. DAY

Barbie Margot and Co. all hang out together on the beach.
It's pretty fun, but not *perfect* fun.

The Barbies play a wicked game of Beach Volleyball while the
Ken's cheer (like reverse Top Gun, _remember this_).

                        ALLAN
            Great cheer, Kens!

Everyone else laughs earnestly but when Barbie Margot tries,
it's forced.

                    BARBIE MARGOT
                (tripping over the laugh)
            Ha, ha. Ha ha ha ha ha.Ha.

Something is wrong. Why can't she _really_ laugh?

                    BARBIE ANA
                (calling out)
            Come on, Barbie, let's run towards
            the water!

Barbie Margot steps up on her tip-toes and wobbles weirdly on
the sand. She can't hold it any longer, her foot cramps and
she topples to the ground. She looks down and discovers that
her feet are - SHOCK! HORROR! - _No longer arched!!!_

She's just got big ole flat feet. She gasps and tries to
crawl herself to the beach bench. Barbie Alexandra, Barbie
Hari, Barbie Sharon, Barbie Emma and Barbie Ana rush over:

                    BARBIE SHARON
            Hey Barbie, are you OK?

                    BARBIE MARGOT
            Yeah, Barbie, I just fell...

        BARBIE HARI   BARBIE MARGOT
    Fell?!   (looking around)
                                I'm so... embarrassed.

                    BARBIE ALEXANDRA
            Barbie doesn't get embarrassed!

                    BARBIE MARGOT
            Barbie, I think my - I don't even
            have any context for this, but - I
            think my feet are - my heels are on
            the ground.

                    BARBIE ANA
            WHAT?!

                    BARBIE MARGOT
            I'm no longer on my tip-toes.

                    BARBIE HARI
            Let me see.
                (gasp!)
            FLAT FEET!!

Barbie Hari throws up nothing. Same with Barbie Alexandra.
Ken Kingsley joins in, throwing up nothing.

                    BARBIE SHARON
          Stop it, Ken.

                    KEN KINGSLEY
                    (nauseous)
          I'm sorry... I'm sorry...

The Barbies ignore him.

                    BARBIE MARGOT
                    (panicking)
          I know I'm Stereotypical Barbie,
          and therefore don't form
          conjectures concerning the
          causality of adjacent unfolding
          events, but some stuff has been
          happening that might be related:
          bad breath this morning, a cold
          shower, burnt waffle, falling off
          my roof...

Barbie Alexandra gasps, hand over mouth.

                    BARBIE ALEXANDRA
          You're malfunctioning!

                    BARBIE MARGOT
          What? No, I'm just, am I?

                    BARBIE EMMA
                    (horrifyingly drawn in)
          I've never *seen* this kind of
          malfunction. It's usually just hair
          related. You know - you're going to
          have to visit... Weird Barbie.

                    BARBIE MARGOT
          But I've *never* had to go visit
          Weird Barbie.

                    BARBIE HARI
          That's because you've never
          malfunctioned.

                    BARBIE SHARON
          I heard that she used to be the
          most beautiful Barbie of all but
          then someone played too hard with
          her in the Real World...

CUT TO: The REAL WORLD with a little girl doing that thing we
all do to our Barbies at some point. She snips off her hair,
colors her face with marker, lights her hair on fire, puts
her in the splits and drop kicks her into her toy bin.

BACK TO: Barbie Margot looking concerned. Barbie Hari is in a trance of the Legend of Weird Barbie:

>   BARBIE HARI
>   ...and now she's fated to an
>   eternity of making other Barbies
>   perfect while falling more and more
>   into disrepair herself. And that we
>   call her Weird Barbie all the time
>   both behind her back and also to
>   her face.
>   (happy again)
>   Anyway, you _have_ to go see her!

>   BARBIE MARGOT
>   Ugh, she's SO Weird. And why is she
>   always in the splits?

EXT/INT. WEIRD BARBIE'S WEIRDHOUSE. DAY

Barbie Margot climbs the seemingly never-ending stairs up to the Weirdhouse. It's like an abstract art version of every girl's Dreamhouse after she's played with it for years. Think Jeff Koons, Gaudi, Murakami all put in a blender.

>   BARBIE MARGOT
>   I would _never_ wear heels if my feet
>   were shaped this way!

Barbie Margot steps gingerly in, looking around.

>   BARBIE MARGOT
>   Um, hello?

Barbie Margot frowns. A dog (Tanner) passes by and poops out little plastic pellets. Barbie Margot steps around them.

>   WEIRD BARBIE (O.S.)
>   (from the dark)
>   What's cookin' good lookin'?

A pool of light illuminates Weird Barbie - she's in the splits, has an unintentionally asymmetrical short haircut and mismatched clothes. She's like David Bowie + a hairless cat.

>   WEIRD BARBIE
>   Welcome, welcome to my Weirdhouse.

Weird Barbie hitches her leg down and lopes oddly into a giant room. Maybe she does a flip or two.

>   WEIRD BARBIE
>   (looking at the floor)
>   Sorry about the dog crap!
>   (MORE)

                    WEIRD BARBIE (CONT'D)
Why anyone would want to introduce
pooping into a doll universe is
beyond me.

                    HELEN MIRREN (V.O.)
          (with distain)
Or pregnancy.

                    WEIRD BARBIE
          (moving on)
What can I do you for?

                    BARBIE MARGOT
          (taking off her heels)
I had to come see you about -- My
feet -- they're um...

                    WEIRD BARBIE
          (looking)
FLAT! HA!
          (with interest)
I've never seen that before...

                    BARBIE MARGOT
Yeah. Can you fix them?

                    WEIRD BARBIE
          (suspicious)
You're Stereotypical Barbie, aren't
you?

                    BARBIE MARGOT
Uh, yeah...

                    WEIRD BARBIE
That Ken of yours is one nice
looking little protein pot.

                    BARBIE MARGOT
Um, I guess.

                    WEIRD BARBIE
I'd love to see what kind of nude
blob he's packing under those
jeans.

She claps her open hands together like the way little kids
mash Barbies together. Barbie Margot watches with horror. It
goes on too long and then stops as suddenly as it started:

                    WEIRD BARBIE
Anyway. What preceded this?

                    BARBIE MARGOT
          Oh, um, nothing. A really fun game
          of volleyball...

                    WEIRD BARBIE
          Really?!

                    BARBIE MARGOT
               (mumbles)
          Thoughts of death.

Weird Barbie looks at her horrified. Small voice:

                    BARBIE MARGOT
          Is that a problem?

                    WEIRD BARBIE
               (concerned)
          Oh.

                    BARBIE MARGOT
          What?

          WEIRD BARBIE   BARBIE MARGOT
Oh.   What?!

                    WEIRD BARBIE
          I'd heard this was possible but
          I've never seen it happen before.

                    BARBIE MARGOT
          Never?!

                    WEIRD BARBIE
          You've opened a portal!

                    BARBIE MARGOT
          I didn't open a portal!

                    WEIRD BARBIE
          Well, someone did! There is a rip
          in the continuum that is the
          membrane between Barbie Land and
          the Real World and if you want to
          be Stereotypical Barbie perfect
          again you've got to go fix it! Or
          you're going to keep going funny.
          Look at your upper thigh.

She does. Ack! A dimple.

                    BARBIE MARGOT
          What is that?!

                    WEIRD BARBIE
          CELLULITE. It'll spread EVERYWHERE
          and you'll start getting mushy and
          sad and... complicated.

                    BARBIE MARGOT
          NO!!! What do I have to do?!?

With that, Weird Barbie turns and travels through her house,
up and over all of the strange architecture. Barbie Margot
tries to keep up.

                    WEIRD BARBIE
          You have to go to the Real World
          and find the girl who is playing
          with you.

                    BARBIE MARGOT
          Playing with me?

Weird Barbie goes through the mess around her, finding a
technical drawing which she refers to briefly and then gets
tired and throws it back on the stack.

                    WEIRD BARBIE
          We're all being played with!
          Usually there's some kind of
          separation: there's the Girl, aka
          the Player, and the Doll, aka the
          Playee. And never the twain shall
          cross.

                    BARBIE MARGOT
          The twain is crossing?

                    WEIRD BARBIE
               (another drawing)
          Yes! The girl playing with you must
          be sad and her thoughts and
          feelings and humanness are
          interfering with your dollness. Am
          I being too technical?

                    BARBIE MARGOT
          Why would she be sad? We fixed
          everything so that all women in the
          real world are happy and powerful!

                    WEIRD BARBIE
          I DON'T KNOW!
               (looking at her hard)
          If you ask me, you're responsible
          for this, too. It usually takes two
          to rip the portal.

                    BARBIE MARGOT
          ME?! But I didn't do anything. I've
          only ever wanted for things to be
          exactly as they are.

                    WEIRD BARBIE
          Well however it happened, you and
          she are becoming inextricably
          intertwined. You have to help her
          to help yourself.

Weird Barbie holds her hands out: this is a Matrix moment
where Barbie Margot is offered two different versions of
life, i.e. red pill and blue pill, except for Weird Barbie
holds a <u>high-heeled shoe</u> in one hand and a <u>Birkenstock sandal</u>
in the other. Very dramatic, full of meaning and moodiness.

                    BARBIE MARGOT
               (re: Birkenstock)
          What is *that?!*

                    WEIRD BARBIE
               (cryptically)
          So what will it be? You can go back
          to the way your life was--
               (holding the high heel up)
          --and not even remember that this
          happened, or you can know the truth
          about the universe.
               (holds up the Birkenstock
                and with a woo-woo voice)
          The question is planted in your
          mind. The choice is yours.

Breaking the "mysterious" spell, Barbie Margot answers
instantly and with too much chipper energy:

                    BARBIE MARGOT
          The first one. The high heel.

                    WEIRD BARBIE
               (annoyed)
          No. We'll do a redo. You're
          supposed to *want* to know!

                    BARBIE MARGOT
               (cheerfully)
          I don't.

                    WEIRD BARBIE
          Babe, listen. You have to want to
          know.

                    BARBIE MARGOT
          I'm not Adventure Barbie, I'm
          Stereotypical Barbie. I'm like the
          Barbie you think of when someone
          says "think of a Barbie" and that's
          me!

                    WEIRD BARBIE
          That is *so sad.*

                    BARBIE MARGOT
               (closes her eyes, happily)
          Okay, I'm ready to forget now.

                    WEIRD BARBIE
          NO!

                    BARBIE MARGOT
               (opening her eyes)
          Why?

                    WEIRD BARBIE
          You're doing this anyway.
          I just gave you a choice so you
          could feel like you're in control!

                    BARBIE MARGOT
          So there is no first option?

                    WEIRD BARBIE
          NO! *You* have to go fix the rip
          yourself. Don't blame me, blame
          Mattel, they make the rules.

                    BARBIE MARGOT
          Ugh, I don't want to go.

                    WEIRD BARBIE
          Fine, get cellulite, I don't care.

Weird Barbie turns away. On Barbie Margot. She summons all
her bravery. She wants to meet the moment.

                    BARBIE MARGOT
               (steels herself)
          Send me through the portal.

Weird Barbie laughs, and then opens a toy-manual.

                    WEIRD BARBIE
          Oh, no, there's no portal to the
          other world. That's just a figure
          of speech.

We see the different vehicles as she rattles off:

                    WEIRD BARBIE
          It's a sports car to a speed boat
          to a rocket ship to a tandem bike
          to a camper van--FUN--to a
          snowmobile--BRR--which will take
          you most of the way to the state of
          Los Angeles where you'll don neon
          and rollerblades and enter the
          country of California. Weird, I
          know. Best if you don't think about
          it too much.

Weird Barbie takes a swig from a flask with nothing in it (of
course), presentation done. After all the energy she now
seems tired of this whole business, and hurries Barbie Margot
out.

                    BARBIE MARGOT
          When I'm there, how do I find this
          girl?

                    WEIRD BARBIE
          You will know.

                    BARBIE MARGOT
          And how will I get back?

                    WEIRD BARBIE
          Same way you came, in reverse.

                    BARBIE MARGOT
          Like I should go forward but do the
          order backward or move backward and
          do the order backward or...?

                    WEIRD BARBIE
               (voice of Zuul)
          REVERSE EVERYTHING.

                    BARBIE MARGOT
          K.

                    WEIRD BARBIE
          If you don't find her and fix
          things, what's ugly will become
          uglier, what's weird will become
          weirder.

Barbie Margot screams.

                    WEIRD BARBIE
          And then you will look like me.

Barbie Margot screams again.

>
                    WEIRD BARBIE
          Gee, thanks. I understand. I set
          myself up for that. Anyway, I
          believe in you.

>   BARBIE MARGOT
                  (flustered)
          Thank you... bye!

EXT. BARBIE DREAMHOUSE/CUL-DE-SAC. MORNING

Barbie Margot's having a send off party with all of the
Barbies - there is a big banner that reads:

**"Bon Voyage to Reality and Good Luck Restoring The Membrane
That Separates Our World From Theirs So You Don't Get
Cellulite!"**

The Kens all stand to the side, a bit like men at a baby
shower. There, but not. Ken Ryan Gosling and Ken Simu do a
jealous mingle.

>   KEN SIMU
          I guess she's going without you.

>   KEN RYAN GOSLING
                  (clearly lying)
          No, she literally asked me, but I
          preferred to stay here.

>   KEN SIMU
                  (provoking)
          Why? Are you *scared*?

>   KEN RYAN GOSLING
          No!

>   KEN SIMU
          I'll bet you're scared and I bet
          she doesn't even want you to go.

>   KEN RYAN GOSLING
          You bet both of those things
          incorrectly! I bet the other
          direction!

>   KEN SIMU
          Which way is that? You don't even
          know.

Barbie gathers around her car with her friends.

                    BARBIE MARGOT
          I just don't want to leave! I'm
          Trying to find reasons not to
          leave!! I'm going to miss you guys
          so much. I just wish someone could
          come with me... but you can't. I
          should do this alone.

Back to the Kens. The other group of Kens are playing a very
mysterious game which appears to be mostly guessing:

                    KEN KINGSLEY
          What bird am I thinking of?

                    KEN NCUTI
          Parrot.

                    KEN SCOTT
          Dolphin. I mean, no, a bird.

                    KEN KINGSLEY
               (pleased)
          PELICAN.

Back to the Barbies: all the Barbies finish bringing her
stuff to the car.

                    BARBIE ALEXANDRA
          We'll miss you Barbie!

                    BARBIE MARGOT
          I'm going to be back in no time
          with perfect feet and we'll forget
          that this *ever* happened.

                    BARBIE EMMA
          And you'll get to see all the good
          work we've done to fix the world.

                    BARBIE ANA
          You'll be such a hero to them!

                    BARBIE SHARON
          All those grateful, powerful women
          who owe their wonderful lives to
          Barbie.

                    BARBIE ALEXANDRA
          I bet every woman will say thank
          you and give you a really big hug!

                    BARBIE MARGOT
               (deep breath)
          Yes! You're right! OK, here I go!
          Bye!

                    BARBIE MERMAID
               (bursting out of the pool)
          Bye Barbie! Good luck in reality!

Barbie Margot hops in her convertible, waving and driving off
into the sunset.

INT. CONVERTIBLE/EXT. BARBIE LAND OPEN ROAD. MORNING

Barbie Margot drives and sings along SUPER LOUD to Indigo
Girls "Closer to Fine," which for some reason they have in
Barbie Land. She's loving this adventure, actually!

                    BARBIE MARGOT
          "I went to the doctor / I went to
          the mountains / I looked to the
          children / I drank from the
          fountains... AHHHHHHH!!!!!

Ken Ryan Gosling pops up in the backseat singing and Barbie
Margot screams her head off and he screams at her screaming.
They skid off the road, flipping over a few times and then
landing upright in the desert.

                    RADIO
               (Indigo Girls still
                singing)
          "Closer I am to Fine..."

Still hysterical:

                    BARBIE MARGOT
          What are you doing here?

                    KEN RYAN GOSLING
          I'm coming with you!

                    BARBIE MARGOT
          Please get out!

                    KEN RYAN GOSLING
          No! I can't! I have a double bet
          with Ken, please, you can't make me
          look uncool in front of Ken!

     BARBIE MARGOT   KEN RYAN GOSLING
Ken's not cool!   HE IS TO ME!

                         BARBIE MARGOT
               You're just going to slow me down!

                         KEN RYAN GOSLING
               What if there's Beach? You'll need
               someone who is a professional in
               that!

                         BARBIE MARGOT
                            (relenting)
               Did you bring your roller blades?

                         KEN RYAN GOSLING
                         (holding them up, smiling)
               I literally go nowhere without
               them.

She thinks, and then relents.

                         BARBIE MARGOT
               OK, let's do this.

                         KEN RYAN GOSLING
                            (so excited)
               Can I sit in front?

                         BARBIE MARGOT
               NO!

He accepts this, and they're OFF! Dramatic music as they go
through all the different kinds of transportation.

                         HELEN MIRREN (V.O.)
               So Barbie and Ken set off on their
               adventure to the Real World!

EXT. TRANSPORTATION

Sports Car - back in their car and on the ROAD! Into...

Speed Boat - Barbie drives the speedboat while Ken hides from
a seagull.

Rocket Ship - Barbie and Ken wear space suits and ride a
rocket, which makes zero sense.

Tandem Bike - through the prairie OR the French Alps? Barbie
on the front of the bike, Ken behind.

Camper Van - In a National Park they screech to a stop, jump
off their bikes, and set up a little grill. Ken flips a
burger while Barbie chills out in a lawn chair, reading a
tabloid.

Snowmobile – BACK TO THE ACTION! – Ken hangs on to Barbie for dear life as she catches air over slaloms.

EXT. VENICE BOARDWALK

Rollerblades – Finally they are in the sunny state of California, in the town of LA, on the boardwalk of Venice Beach – wearing rollerblades.

Barbie Margot wears a bikini and Ken wears a onesie. They're openly getting a lot of looks. Just the two of them in REAL Los Angeles is genuinely strange and hilarious. They appear as extremely good-looking aliens.

> BARBIE MARGOT
> Wow! The Real World!

Ken smiles and waves loving all of this, but Barbie Margot looks confused bordering on anxious.

Note: this is more real than Barbie Land but still heightened, like a 1980s comedy – slightly exaggerated. Like there is no way Ferris Bueller sang the Beatles at that German parade, but we allow it because it's fun. Same here.

> KEN RYAN GOSLING
> See, I told you there'd be Beach!

> BEACH DUDE
> (hollering at her)
> Give us a smile, blondie.

People are laughing and pointing and amused and also leering.

> BARBIE MARGOT
> What's going on, why are all these
> men looking at me?

> KEN RYAN GOSLING
> They're also looking at ME!

Ken winks at someone who winks back.

> KEN RYAN GOSLING
> I LOVE THIS!

> BARBIE MARGOT
> (looking worried)
> I feel kind of ill-at-ease, I don't
> even know the word for it... Like
> I'm conscious of it but it's my
> self I'm conscious of--

                    KEN RYAN GOSLING
                (happy as a clam)
            I'm not getting any of that. I feel
            appreciated but not ogled. Mine has
            no undertone of violence.

                    BARBIE MARGOT
            Mine *very much* has an undertone of
            violence.

Up ahead is a construction site, workers on break for lunch.

                    BARBIE MARGOT
            Oh, great! A construction site! We
            need that good feminine energy.

But as they get closer, it's not what she thought.
Construction workers eat sandwiches and cat-call Barbie.

    CONSTRUCTION WORKER 1   CONSTRUCTION WORKER 3
Do fries come with that   Have I died and gone to
shake?   heaven because you're an
                                angel.

    CONSTRUCTION WORKER 2   CONSTRUCTION WORKER 4
If I said you had a hot body,   Is that a mirror in your
would you hold it against me?   pocket? 'Cause I can see
                                myself in your pants!

                    BARBIE MARGOT
            I don't know _exactly_ what you meant
            by all those little quips, but I'm
            picking up on some sort of entendre
            which appears to be double, and I
            would just like to inform you that
            I don't have a vagina and he--
                (pointing at Ken)
            --doesn't have a penis. We don't
            have genitals

The Construction Workers look at them blankly and then shrug,
unbothered. This is Los Angeles after all, live and let live!

                    CONSTRUCTION WORKERS
            Far out!... That's okay... Whatever
            works... you do you...

They're actually very sweet guys. She blades away as Ken Ryan
Gosling tries to impress the construction workers.

                    KEN RYAN GOSLING
            I have all the genitals.

He catches up to Barbie Margot.

                    BARBIE MARGOT
          Jeez, you would think a
          construction site at lunchtime
          would be the perfect place for a
          little woman-power. But this one
          was so... male.

                    KEN RYAN GOSLING
               (a little excited)
          Yeah everything is almost, like,
          reversed, here.

There's a *slight* moment here. Like maybe he's ON to
something... But they're distracted as they pass a large
billboard advertising The Miss Universe Contest:

                    BARBIE MARGOT
          Look, the Supreme Court!

                    KEN RYAN GOSLING
          They're so smart!

Another Beach dude passes by and slaps Barbie Margot on the
ass. Barbie Margot punches him in the face. Ken screams.

INT. VENICE CENTRAL BOOKING. DAY

Barbie Margot and Ken Ryan Gosling's mug shots.

Then they are being finger printed. Over and over again
because the cops can't find any prints. The cops drool over
Barbie Margot:

                    POLICEMAN
          I love me a leotard.

                    POLICEMAN #2
          I love the elbow pads.

                    BARBIE MARGOT
               (to Ken)
          I think we should get some
          different clothes.

EXT. VENICE BEACH STOREFRONT. DAY.

Ken Ryan Gosling exits wearing all denim with fringe and a
cowboy hat, followed by Barbie Margot, who wears a pink
cowgirl outfit. ALL the security lights and bells go, but
they are oblivious.

                    BARBIE MARGOT
          We look great!

                    KEN RYAN GOSLING
                 (admiring his reflection)
          I LOVE FRINGE!

                    BARBIE MARGOT
          I love denim!

A Security Guard rushes after them, panicked.

                    SECURITY GUARD
          Hey! You two! What are you doing?!
          You have to pay for those!

They give chase!

INT. VENICE CENTRAL BOOKING. AGAIN. DAY

Barbie Margot and Ken Ryan, getting finger printed. The male
cops are *still* leering.

                    POLICE MAN #2
          She's even *sexier* in clothes.

                    POLICE MAN
          I know, because you can imagine
          more.

                    POLICE MAN #2
          You know what? Keep 'em!

                    BARBIE MARGOT
          Goddammit!

EXT. POLICE STATION. DAY

Barbie Margot and Ken Ryan Gosling emerge into the midday LA
sun, wearing their stolen/gifted clothes.

                    BARBIE MARGOT
          Weird Barbie said I'd know how to
          find this girl, but I have NO IDEA.
                 (takes a deep breath)
          What would a smart Barbie do? I
          just need to clear my mind so I can
          think.

Barbie sits down on a bench, almost like she's meditating.

                    KEN RYAN GOSLING
                 (annoyed)
          I hate it when people *think*. I'm so
          bored!

                    BARBIE MARGOT
          The faster I figure this out, the
          faster we get home.

She closes her eyes. Ken Ryan Gosling gets all antsy like a
kid, unable to sit still.

                    KEN RYAN GOSLING
                 (lost without her)
          What am I supposed to do?!

                    BARBIE MARGOT
          Go for a walk or something!

He makes faces, then goes for a walk.

                    BARBIE MARGOT
                 (eyes still closed)
          Don't go far!

EXT. CENTURY CITY. DAY.

Ken Ryan Gosling walks under a sign for: CENTURY CITY. He
looks up: A tall building looms over him and he starts
putting together the world a little bit. He sees:

- A gym, full of men.

- A man in a mink.

- A policeman on a horse.

- A Hummer, stuffed to the brim with businessmen.

- Generic men in business suits shaking hands having generic
business conversations.

                    BUSINESSMEN
          Great deal. Great deal. We're all
          going to make a lot of money.

A female secretary tries to come up and tell her boss
something, he holds up his hand to stop her:

                    BUSINESSMEN
          In a second, Margaret.
                 (to his associates)
          Shall we all shake on it?

She backs away, submissive, as they all shake madly. Ken Ryan
cannot believe what he's seeing. Are they more powerful than
she is?? How is this possible?

Ken Ryan Gosling rides an escalator up to a giant video screen, playing images of Big Man Stuff:

- Money, Presidents, Golf videos, mini-fridges, a bunch of dudes working out at the gym. Men in sports, men as statues, men in paintings, important men in photographs, the Greased Lightening scene from Grease, all culminating in Sylvester Stallone in a mink coat.

- MEN EVERYWHERE and then just another horse and then MORE MEN EVERYWHERE!

EXT. POLICE STATION. DAY

Barbie Margot still sitting on the bench, breathes in and out, and sees:

Glimpses of A Girl, maybe a pigtail, some chipped nail polish. She's "Shining" or something like that. But without the horror!

- The Girl laughing with her Mom, eating ice cream.

- The Girl opening the door saying "Mom, I had a bad dream."

- The Girl playing Barbies with her Mom - her Mom shows her a Barbie idea sketch and the girl applauds.

- The Girl is getting older, moving away when her Mom tries to show affection.

- The Girl plops a box of her Barbies and Barbie accessories in front of her Mom, clearly marked "Goodwill."

- The Mom sadly drops her daughter off at school, and when she tries to wave at her, the Girl pretends not to see her. It's junior high. Everyone is their worst self in junior high.

CLOSE on Barbie Margot, a tear rolls down her face.

Barbie opens her eyes. She wipes the tear from her face. She looks down at the moisture in her hand. She's never cried before.

                    BARBIE MARGOT
                 (to herself)
            That felt achy... but good.

Barbie Margot looks around - across the street she sees a park, filled with mundane and beautiful and funny and sad moments of every day life.

- A young couple with a baby.

- Kids playing tag.

- A teen girl crying and being comforted by another girl.

- Best friends laughing together.

- A middle aged couple walking hand in hand.

- Three friends in an argument.

- An old man feeds the birds.

- Someone reading a book.

- A man with a child.

- Guys kicking a ball around.

- 20-somethings arguing.

- A young man who looks like he's been crying.

Next to her an Older Woman sits on a bench, reading. Barbie
studies her for a moment.

Barbies don't get old, so this is something she doesn't have
experience with. The woman, as if she can feel Barbie's gaze
on her, looks up. They meet eyes. The Older Woman nods in
greeting.

>   BARBIE MARGOT
>   You're so beautiful.

>   OLDER WOMAN
>   (cheeky)
>   I know it.

They laugh, it's lovely.

Ken runs up to her, breaking the moment.

>   KEN RYAN GOSLING (O.S.)
>   BARBIE!

She turns to him, and he and Barbie excitedly say:

>   KEN RYAN GOSLING   BARBIE MARGOT
> I've got it!   I've got it!

>   KEN RYAN GOSLING
>   What have you got?

>   BARBIE MARGOT
>   You go first.

                    KEN RYAN GOSLING
          No you!

                    BARBIE MARGOT
          Let's go at the same time.

          KEN RYAN GOSLING   BARBIE MARGOT
Men rule the world!   She's at school!

                    BARBIE MARGOT
          What was that?

                    KEN RYAN GOSLING
           The girl is at school!

          BARBIE MARGOT   KEN RYAN GOSLING
But what did you ? --   -- Nothing, doesn't matter,
                                  let's go to the SCHOOL!

They both run off together, and Barbie sneaks a glance back,
but the old woman is back to reading her newspaper, the
moment has passed.

EXT. MATTEL HEADQUARTERS. DAY.

An imposing, many floored building. Masculine. STRONG.

A phone is ringing from somewhere. We BOOM DOWN from the top
floor ALL THE WAY DOWN --

INT. MATTEL HEADQUARTERS LOWEST FLOOR. DAY.

An endless forest of cubicles.

                    MATTEL EMPLOYEE
          Hello?

Split screen with:

INT. FBI HEADQUARTERS. DAY.

Men in those aviators for no reason, pictures on cork boards.

                    DAN AT THE FBI
          This is Dan at the FBI.

                    MATTEL EMPLOYEE
          This is Aaron at Mattel.

                    DAN AT THE FBI
          I don't give a flying squirrel who
          you are Aaron! What are you, like
          an intern?

          AARON DINKINS   DAN AT THE FBI
I mean, not really an--   Two of your dolls have gotten
                              loose!

               AARON DINKINS
        Impossible. How do you know?

               DAN AT THE FBI
        Don't sass me Aaron! Couple of
        blondes answering to Barbie and Ken
        rollerblading in Santa Monica.
        Claim to have no genitals.

               AARON DINKINS
        Genital-less?

               DAN AT THE FBI
        We're going to need Mattel's help
        landing the eagle. Don't crap the
        bed, Aaron!

               AARON DINKINS
           (concerned)
        I won't.

Sweating bullets, he hangs up the phone.

               AARON DINKINS
        This is bad. This is really bad.

Another younger employee peers over the top of his cubicle:

           YOUNGER MATTEL EMPLOYEE
        What?!

               AARON DINKINS
        This happened once before.

Popping up from ANOTHER cubicle, three cubicles away:

        AN EVEN YOUNGER MATTEL EMPLOYEE
        What?! When?!

               AARON DINKINS
         About ten years ago a woman named
        Skipper turned up in Key West at
        some family's home and asked to
        babysit the kids... She then tried
        to take their toddler surfing. We
        were able to straighten it out and
        keep it under wraps.
           (grave)
        But this is serious.

                    AARON DINKINS
          I'm going all the way up.

                    YOUNGER MATTEL EMPLOYEE
          No one goes all the way up! You may
          never come back!

                    AARON DINKINS
          I know.

INT. MATTEL HEADQUARTERS. ELEVATOR.

He takes a deep breath and steps into the elevator. Floors
tick by 99, 100, 101. Walks briskly down a huge hallway.

INT. MATTEL HEADQUARTERS. BOARDROOM RECEPTION.

CLOSE on some sketches of Barbie. But these Barbies look
distressed, mascara running down her cheeks from crying. She
wears the identical clothes to Barbie Margot.

A woman, Gloria, sits at a reception desk. She's in her late
30s, but has something of the kid in her, a pair of pink
shoes? We love her! _She_ is drawing the sketch.

Gloria has an old Barbie on her desk which _resembles Barbie_
Margot. And next to that a _photo of her daughter._ She's
singing "Closer to Fine" to herself.

Aaron stops at the desk. Gloria is so lost in her drawing she
doesn't see him. He clears his throat.

                    AARON DINKINS
          Um... Gloria.

He snaps his fingers. She shakes her head and looks at him.

                    GLORIA
          Oh, hi, Aaron.

                    AARON DINKINS
               (re: her sketch)
          New designs?

                    GLORIA
          Yeah, for some reason I just
          started drawing her. I don't know
          why.

She hands them to him.

                         GLORIA
          It's Crippling Shame Barbie,
          Irrepressible Thoughts of Death
          Barbie, Full Body Cellulite Barbie.

                      AARON DINKINS
          Yeah, OK.
               (getting to the point)
          I have to talk to the top brass.

                   RECEPTIONIST/GLORIA
          They're in a big corporate ideas
          sesh. No one is to be admitted--

But Aaron is walking toward the door.

                   RECEPTIONIST/GLORIA
               (stage whisper)
          AARON stop it!...

INT. MATTEL HEADQUARTERS. BOARDROOM

He opens a door to a giant PINK GLITTERY board room. It's
like the inside of a 5 year old girl's sparkly heart.

                       MATTEL CEO
               (true believer)
          Always be empowering girls! Always!
          What do we really sell? We sell
          dreams! Imagination! And sparkle!
          When you think of sparkle, what do
          you think after that?

He doesn't wait for an answer, already so pumped to say:

                       MATTEL CEO
          Female agency.

                      AARON DINKINS
          Um... excuse me...

A table of men turns around all at once. They're all wearing
suits but it somehow feels like tuxedos.

                       MATTEL CEO
          Who are you?

                      AARON DINKINS
          Aaron Dinkins, sir.

                       MATTEL CEO
          We're in the middle of a major sit-
          down here, Aaron Dinkins.

                    AARON DINKINS
          But, I think you're going to want
          to hear this, sir.

                    MATTEL CEO
          Can you just email it? And you can
          send it to me EOD
               (proud)
          End of day.

                    AARON DINKINS
          May I put it in a whisper, sir?

                    MATTEL CEO
          Ugh, fine, whisper me.

Aaron Dinkins leans in and whispers something to the Mattel
Executive #1. He's *ashen*. He turns and whispers to the man
next to him and each man in turn reacts and whispers to the
man next to him. Finally, the CEO listens with shock:

                    MATTEL CEO
          My god it's a repeat of Skipper in
          Key West.

                    AARON DINKINS
          And with all due respect, that was
          Skipper, sir. This is...
               (dramatically)
          Barbie.

They all react. The Mattel CEO stands up, dramatically.

                    MATTEL CEO
          If this got out, that our dolls
          were coming to Los Angeles from
          Barbie Land as life-size versions
          of themselves and roaming the earth
          it would be very bad...
               (lame finish)
          ... for business.

CUT TO: Gloria listens outside the conference room doors. She
shakes her head, doing some insane calculation.

                    GLORIA
               (to herself)
          Barbie? In the real world?
               (thinks)
          No, that's impossible.
               (thinks again)
          Right?

We CUT BACK inside the BOARD ROOM:

                    MATTEL EXECUTIVE #2
          We've got a definite situation on
          our hands.

                    MATTEL CEO
          Catastrophic! I can't stress that
          enough! What's your name again?

                    AARON DINKINS
          Uh, Aaron Dinkins Sir

                    MATTEL CEO
          Aaron Dickinson?

                    AARON DINKINS
          Dinkins. Um, is Barbie Land like an
          alternate reality or like our
          imaginations come to life or...?

                    ALL OF THE EXECUTIVES
          Yes.

                    MATTEL CEO
          Think of it as a town in Sweden,
          Aaron Dinkins.
               (sizing him up)
          How much do you weigh? Never mind.
          This sounds like a job for the box.

                    ALL OF THE EXECUTIVES
          Yes sir.

                    MATTEL CEO
          No one rests until this doll is
          back in a box!

EXT. JUNIOR HIGH SCHOOL. AFTERNOON

Barbie Margot and Ken Ryan Gosling approach the school.
Barbie Margot sticks out even more here, as the kids are all
wearing dark colors trying not to be noticed. You know,
Junior High School.

                    BARBIE MARGOT
               (looking up at the sign)
          Look! Davey Crocket Junior High
          School! Just like I saw in my
          vision.

                    KEN RYAN GOSLING
          A man on a horse!

                         BARBIE MARGOT
               We better find her soon, I've
               started to get all these weirdo
               FEELINGS. Ugh. Like I have fear
               with no specific object, what's
               that?

                         MOM
                    (passing by)
               Anxiety. I have it too.
                    (re: the kids)
               They're just awful at this age.

                         KEN RYAN GOSLING
               I feel _amazing_.

                         MOM
               That's because kids don't take it
               out on Dads.

                         KEN RYAN GOSLING
               Cool!

Kids are running everywhere. Barbie Margot and Ken Ryan
Gosling try to not look sketchy.

                         BARBIE MARGOT
               She's *got* to be here somewhere.

They pass the library and Ken says, kind of suspiciously:

                         KEN RYAN GOSLING
               Hey, I'm just going to pop into to
               the library and see if I can find
               any books on trucks...

                         BARBIE MARGOT
               Okay, but don't get in trouble!

                         KEN RYAN GOSLING
               I won't!

EXT. JUNIOR HIGH SCHOOL. CAFETERIA

Barbie scans all the different girls' faces and then BAM -
like Roy Scheider in "JAWS" seeing that kid getting eaten -
she sees her Girl, the one from her vision!

Her Girl is sitting in a VERY prominent table with a group of
other pretty 13 year old girls. She's clearly popular. They
all have Hydroflasks, big t-shirts, scrunchies, Mario Badescu
Or whatever kids are into after this pandemic!

She begins to walk towards the girl but is interrupted by:

                         OTHER GIRL
                   What are you doing?

Indicating the one she thinks is HER girl:

                         BARBIE MARGOT
                   What's that girl's name?

                         OTHER GIRL
                        (reverence)
                   That's Sasha.

                         BARBIE MARGOT
                        (calling out)
                   Hey Sasha!

                         OTHER GIRL
                        (panicking)
                   NO DON'T TALK TO HER! Sasha can
                   talk to you but you can *never* talk
                   to Sasha. She'll crush you.

                         BARBIE MARGOT
                   Don't worry - everyone likes me and
                   thinks I'm cool and pretty.

                         OTHER GIRL
                        (staring at her)
                   Huh.

                         BARBIE MARGOT
                   Thank you!

And then she goes up to talk to Sasha, and all these 13-year-
old queen bees turn to look at her. NOTE: this is the
opposite of what Barbie (and we!) think will happen.

                         BARBIE MARGOT
                   Hey ladies! Sasha, what's up?

Sasha and her friends stare at Barbie Margot, stunned:

                         SASHA
                        (if looks could kill...)
                   Who are you?

                         BARBIE MARGOT
                   I'm only your favorite woman of all
                   time - Barbie!

                         SASHA
                   You really think you're *Barbie?!*

                    BARBIE MARGOT
          Well yeah!

They burst out with lots of mean laughter, unable to stop.

          POPULAR GIRL #1   POPULAR GIRL #2
Omg she's *crazy.*   Do you think she's escaped
                                from an insane asylum?

          POPULAR GIRL #3   POPULAR GIRL #2
So do you think you're like   Tell us more about how you
pretty?   think you're *Barbie.*

                    SASHA
          Okay, so you're like BARBIE Barbie.
          Like a professional bimbo?

                    BARBIE MARGOT
          No way! Barbie's not a bimbo!
          Barbie's a lawyer. And a doctor.
          And a senator. And a Nobel Prize
          winner.

                    POPULAR GIRL #1
          You're a Nobel Prize winner?

                    BARBIE MARGOT
               (slightly defensive)
          Well, not me. But *Barbie* is.

They all laugh in her face, again. Barbie is confused:

                    BARBIE MARGOT
          Don't you guys - I mean aren't you
          guys going to thank me and give me
          a big hug? For being your FAVORITE
          toy?

                    SASHA
          We haven't played with Barbies
          since we were like 5 years old.

                    POPULAR GIRL #2
          Yeah. I hated dolls with hair.

                    POPULAR GIRL #1
          I played with Barbie but it was the
          last resort.

                    POPULAR GIRL #3
          I loved Barbie...

They give that girl a *look.*

                    SASHA
          Anyways. Even then it was horrible
          for us.

                    BARBIE MARGOT
          Horrible? Why?

Her friends egg her on, they know that Sasha can totally
flatten someone.

          POPULAR GIRL #2   POPULAR GIRL #1
Come, on Sasha.   Give it to her.

                    POPULAR GIRL #3
          Destroy Barbie.

                    SASHA
          Ok, **Barbie**, let's do this.

Sasha's verbal jabs are like a boxer relentlessly landing
punches in a ring, maybe we even shoot it like Raging Bull.
She is clearly *so* smart and *so* articulate that you can't help
but admire her.

                    SASHA
          You've been making women feel bad
          about themselves since you were
          invented.

                    BARBIE MARGOT
          No, I think you have that the wrong
          way around.

                    SASHA
          You represent everything wrong with
          our culture: sexualized capitalism,
          unrealistic physical ideals.

                    BARBIE MARGOT
          Whoa hang on you're describing
          something stereotypical. Barbie is
          so much more than that.

                    SASHA
          Look at yourself!

                    BARBIE MARGOT
               (she has a point)
          Well, I am, actually, Stereotypical
          Barbie.

                    SASHA
          You set the feminist movement back
          fifty years, you destroy girls'
          innate sense of worth and you're
          killing the planet with your
          glorification of rampant
          consumerism.

                    BARBIE MARGOT
          But, but I'm supposed to help you
          and make you happy and powerful –

                    SASHA
          – I *am* powerful and until you
          showed up here and declared
          yourself "Barbie", I hadn't thought
          about you in *years*, you FASCIST.

Barbie bursts into tears and runs away. The Other Girl
watches Barbie run, and just shakes her head.

                    THE OTHER GIRL
          They never listen.

We stay with Sasha for a moment, who suddenly feels bad.
Under all the bravado is a lot of feeling.

EXT. JUNIOR HIGH SCHOOL.

MEANWHILE: Ken runs out of the school library with a bunch of
books in his arms – Men & Wars, The Origins of the
Patriarchy, Why Men Rule (Literally) and just one called
Horses. His mind is blown.

A Female Pedestrian stops and asks, casually:

                    FEMALE PEDESTRIAN
          Excuse me, sir, do you have the
          time?

                    KEN RYAN GOSLING
               (stunned)
          You respect me!

                    FEMALE PEDESTRIAN
          Um, do you know what time it is?

                    KEN RYAN GOSLING
          No, I do not!

                    FEMALE PEDESTRIAN
          Thank you?

Ken feels like he was just declared king.

                    KEN RYAN GOSLING
          Why didn't Barbie tell me about
          Patriarchy? Which, according to my
          understanding, is where men and
          horses run everything!
                    (inspired)
          I shall seek my fortune there!

QUICK IMPOSSIBLE MONTAGE:

INT. OFFICE BUILDING

Ken Ryan Gosling addresses a businessman.

                    KEN RYAN GOSLING
          I want a high level, high paying
          job with influence.

                    OFFICE EMPLOYEE
          You need at least an MBA and many
          of our people have PhDs.

                    KEN RYAN GOSLING
          Isn't being a man enough???

                    OFFICE EMPLOYEE
          Actually right now it's the
          opposite.

                    KEN RYAN GOSLING
          But that's not what books say! You
          guys certainly aren't doing
          patriarchy well.

                    OFFICE EMPLOYEE
               (winks at Ken)
          Oh, we're doing it well. We just
          hide it better now.

INT. DOCTORS OFFICE

We watch Ken also get rejected from a DOCTOR'S OFFICE.

                    FEMALE DOCTOR
          No, I won't let you do "just one
          appendectomy!"

                    KEN RYAN GOSLING
          BUT I'M A MAN!

                    FEMALE DOCTOR
          But not a doctor.

                    KEN RYAN GOSLING
          Please?!

                    FEMALE DOCTOR
          No.

                    KEN RYAN GOSLING
          Can I talk to a doctor?

                    FEMALE DOCTOR
          You are talking to a doctor.

                    KEN RYAN GOSLING
          Can you get me a coffee? And I need
          a clicky pen and a white coat and a
          sharp thing!
                    (sees a man)
          There he is! Doctor!

EXT. VENICE BEACH

And even from a BEACH. A life-guard listens, perplexed.

                    KEN RYAN GOSLING
          I would like to apply for the job
          of Beach.

                    LIFE-GUARD
          Oh so you want to be a life guard?

                    KEN RYAN GOSLING
          Oh I'm not trained to go over
          <u>there</u>.
                    (points to the water)
          I'm trained to stand confidently
          over here.

He points to the sand at his feet.

                    LIFE-GUARD
          But nobody is in danger <u>here</u>.

                    KEN RYAN GOSLING
                    (proudly)
          And even if they were I'm not
          trained to save them.

Ken trudges away, rejected by the life-guard.

                    KEN RYAN GOSLING
          I can't even do BEACH here!

Clutching his books, he returns to the school.

EXT. JUNIOR HIGH SCHOOL

Barbie Margot is sitting in the parking lot still fully
weeping from her interaction with Sasha.

> BARBIE MARGOT
> (to herself, baffled)
> She thinks I'm a fascist? I don't
> control the railways or the flow of
> commerce??

Ken Ryan has arrived back at the school and approaches the
same Female Pedestrian, now with her tween daughter. She's
not thrilled to see him again.

> KEN RYAN GOSLING
> There you are, that went terrible.
> I need a place where I can start
> patriarchy fresh.

Barbie Margot is approached by bunch of CIA or FBI-looking
types - dark suits, mirrored sunglasses, earpieces, but
emblazoned with the Mattel Logo.

> MATTEL AGENT
> Miss Barbie?

> BARBIE MARGOT
> (sniffling)
> It's just Barbie.

> MATTEL AGENT
> You're going to have to come with
> us.

Ken watches from a distance. He freezes.

> BARBIE MARGOT
> Who are you?

> MATTEL AGENT
> We're Mattel.

> KEN RYAN GOSLING
> (to himself)
> Mattel!

> BARBIE MARGOT
> OH THANK GOODNESS! I've got to talk
> to someone in charge. It's all
> backwards here. Men look at me like
> I'm an object, girls hate me,
> everyone thinks I'm crazy and I
> keep getting arrested.

                    MATTEL AGENT
          Just step this way, ma'am.

                    BARBIE MARGOT
          I also just learned how to cry!
          First I got one tear and then I got
          a bunch...

She keeps talking as Ken has a little conversation with the
Female Pedestrian.

                    KEN RYAN GOSLING
          What do I do? Should I go after
          Barbie into that scary unmarked
          black truck car?
               (to himself)
          A truck car I would like to have
          actually...
               (back to the pedestrian)
          Nah, she'll be fine, it's Mattel!
               (excited)
          I know! I'll go back to Barbie
          Land. Wait until I tell the Kens
          what I've learned! Oh it's going to
          be beautiful!
               (sotto)
          Back to Barbie Land!

                    FEMALE PEDESTRIAN
               (walking away)
          Let's go... that way.

Ken hurries off... And Sasha gets into her Mom's car. It's
Gloria, the receptionist from Mattel! Now we get it!

                    GLORIA
          Hi Honey Bear!

                    SASHA
          MOM! Don't call me that!

                    GLORIA
          Shoot, sorry! I got off early
          because of a crisis at work. I
          thought we could go get soft serve
          this afternoon!

Gloria and Sasha see Barbie Margot getting into the van:

                    SASHA
               (unleashes the teen)
          Thank god they arrested that nut
          job!
               (checking herself)
                    (MORE)

                        SASHA (CONT'D)
          I mean: that reality-challenged
          woman. She thinks she's Barbie--

                        GLORIA
                   (can't believe it)
          Wait, what did you say?

CLOSE on Gloria's face - WHAT?! It's 1/2 of the "love look":
she <u>recognizes</u> her. But although Gloria can see Barbie
Margot, Barbie Margot can't see Gloria.

... as one of the Mattel employees shuts the doors on
Barbie's friendly face, and looks around all secret-agent-
like as he gets into the passenger seat and they drive off.

EXT./INT. BLACK VAN. DAY

As the van zooms down the highway, a chipper Barbie tries to
talk to the men in the car.

                        BARBIE MARGOT
          Of course, Mattel! It was *you guys*
          who wanted me to come to the Real
          World! Because it definitely wasn't
          that Sasha girl.

No one responds.

EXT. GIANT MATTEL HEADQUARTERS. DAY

The scary black van pulls up, and Barbie steps out looking up
at the giant building.

                        BARBIE MARGOT
          Thanks for the ride! This has been
          so much fun.

She is escorted through the big double doors...

                        BARBIE MARGOT
                   (in awe)
          Wow! The Mothership!

INT. MATTEL HEADQUARTERS. LOBBY

Barbie Margot smiles as she's taken through the lobby and up
a glass elevator and it opens on to the top floor with all
the executives... And she opens the door on So Much Pink.

INT. MATTEL HEADQUARTERS. BOARDROOM.

                  1/2 EXECUTIVES ALL TOGETHER
          Barbie! We're so happy to see you!

                    THE OTHER HALF ALL TOGETHER
            Can we get you anything? Mineral
            water?

                    BARBIE MARGOT
            Yes, thank you.

She's handed a glass of mineral water which she turns and
pours all over her open mouth and down her shirt. The lime
wedge sticking to her cheek. They all stare at her.

                    BARBIE MARGOT
                (inspecting the glass)
            I'm not used to that having
            anything in it.

The executives part, revealing our CEO, arms outstretched.

                    MATTEL CEO
            We've been REALLY anxious to get
            some quality face time with you...

                    BARBIE MARGOT
            Of COURSE! So what can I do to
            repair the rift in the space time
            continuum portal and get my feet
            back and that one cellulite gone?
            And generally just not turn into
            Weird Barbie.

They all look at her blankly.

                    MATTEL CEO
            We have been discussing that very
            topic. If you are agreeable to it,
            we would love it if you could
            just... get into this giant box.

A human-size Barbie box is wheeled out. It has the logo and
plastic restraining straps and everything.

                    MATTEL CEO
            If you get in that box, you'll go
            back to Barbie Land, and everything
            will be as it was.

Barbie thinks for a minute. The executives all impatiently
lean forward. It's taking everything for them not to just
capture her and put her in the box themselves.

                    BARBIE MARGOT
                (finally)
            You know what. We should probably
            get Ken first.

                    MATTEL CEO
          Ken?

                    BARBIE MARGOT
          You know... Ken.

                    MATTEL CEO
          Oh Ken! The guy. Oh right!

WE CUT BACK TO: Ken just screaming his lungs out on the
rocket going back the other direction.

BACK TO MATTEL:

                    MATTEL CEO
          ... yeah, Ken isn't something we're
          worried about... ever.

                    BARBIE MARGOT
          OK. I'll get in the box.

                    EXECUTIVES ALL TOGETHER
               (relieved)
          Oh, wonderful!

                    BARBIE MARGOT
          But since I came all the way here
          could I meet the woman in charge?
          Your CEO?

They all hesitate. The male Mattel CEO raises his hand.

                    MATTEL CEO
          Um, that would be me.

                    BARBIE MARGOT
          Well what about the CFO?

But it's another man.

                    EXECUTIVE #3
          Er, me.

                    BARBIE MARGOT
          The COO?

Man.

                    EXECUTIVE #2
          Me here.

                    BARBIE MARGOT
          Goodness gracious, what about --
          President of the Barbie division.

It's another man.

                    EXECUTIVE #1   AARON DINKINS
Present.   Um, I'm a man with no power,
                                             does that make me a woman?

                         BARBIE MARGOT
               ARE THERE ANY WOMEN IN CHARGE?!

                         MATTEL CEO
                    (emotional)
               Listen, I know where you're going
               with this, and I have to say I
               really resent it because we are a
               company literally MADE of women.
               There was a woman CEO in the 90's
               and another one at some other time.
               Women are the freaking foundation
               of this long phallic building! We
               have gender neutral bathrooms up
               the wazoo! Every single one of
               these men you see before you loves
               women.

                         EXECUTIVES IN UNISON
               Up the wazoo!

                         MATTEL CEO
               I am the son of a mother, I am the
               mother of a son, I am the nephew of
               a woman aunt, some of my best
               friends are Jewish... what I'm
               trying to say is GET IN THE BOX YOU
               JEZEBEL!

Everyone gasps!

                         MATTEL CEO
               What?! I can't say JEZEBEL now?!

Barbie Margot seems unfazed, looks at the box.

                         BARBIE MARGOT
               I haven't been in a box in ages.

One executive steps into the box and then jumps back out.

                         MATTEL CEO
               See it's easy.

                         BARBIE MARGOT
               OK.

She slowly steps into the box.

                    BARBIE MARGOT
          I totally remember this smell! I'm
          having a real Proustian flashback.

                    EXECUTIVES ALL TOGETHER
          Haha, Proust!

                    MATTEL CEO
                (to his neighbor)
          Remember Proust Barbie? That did
          not sell well.

The employees surround the box somewhat menacingly. A Mattel
Employee grabs the plastic ties from the holes in the back of
the box and pulls.

Barbie Margot feels the restraints tighten on her wrist. She
hesitates, it sinking in. She pulls her wrist out quickly
just as the plastic cinches. Then she jumps out of the box.

                    BARBIE MARGOT
          You know what? Before I get in the
          box, can I just make sure my hair
          is perfect?

                    MATTEL CEO
          It really is time to get in the
          box!

                    BARBIE MARGOT
          But I want to look *factory*
          beautiful.

                    MATTEL CEO
          OK, but let's hurry it up.

She backs over toward the bathroom and then zigs toward the
double doors of the conference room. Then she BOLTS!

                    MATTEL CEO
          Get that Barbie!

INT. MATTEL CUBICLES. CONTINUOUS.

A BIG CHASE through the main bullpen offices of Mattel. The
CEO and all the executives hurry after her. It's like a giant
maze. Barbie Margot darts around the cubicles as employees
work, people pass from cubicle to cubicle popping up and
looking around, trying to spot her.

                    MATTEL CEO
                (to the troops)
          It's quicker if you go OVER the
          cubicles!

The CEO tries to scramble/climb badly over the TOP of a
cubicle and topples into an employee and a computer console.

Barbie sprints toward giant double doors on the other side of
the room. The Mattel Executives in hot pursuit. She hurries
through the doors and shoves a broom through the handles to
hold them off.

Barbie enters a big hallway with lots of doors, she tries
every one, but they're all locked. Trapped! Panicked! She
hears the executives getting closer. Then one door opens...

INT. MAGICAL ROOM FROM THE 1950S. ETERNITY

She enters the room and shuts the door behind her.

                    A VOICE (O.S.)
          Oh, hello, come in.

Barbie Margot sees a woman, dressed like a mom in the 1950's.
The room we see resembles a 1950's kitchen. She's working on
something - her sewing machine is out, and there are scraps
of paper and cloth all over the kitchen table.

                    1950 WOMAN
          Don't worry, you're safe here.

                    BARBIE MARGOT
                (looking around)
          What is this place?

                    1950 WOMAN
                (laughing at herself)
          I always find that I think best at
          kitchen tables. Tea?

                    BARBIE MARGOT
          Yes, please.

The woman hands her the cup, which Barbie Margot brings to
her lips then hesitates. A little dribbles down her chin but
she is able to drink it too. She smiles, proud of herself.
She feels strangely comfortable here.

                    BARBIE MARGOT
          So, a woman does work here.

                    1950 WOMAN
          Oh, sweetie, we do more than work
          here.

                    BARBIE MARGOT
                 (comfortable)
          The real world isn't what I thought
          it was.

                    1950 WOMAN
                 (smiling)
          It never is. And isn't that
          marvelous?

There is a moment that passes between them. Barbie Margot
feels the woman's gaze.

                    BARBIE MARGOT
          What? Is it that I don't know how
          to drink tea?

                    1950 WOMAN
          No. You look different.

                    BARBIE MARGOT
                 (embarrassed)
          I'm not what I used to be. I used
          to be perfect.

                    1950 WOMAN
          I don't know, I think you're just
          right.

She settles down at her sewing machine and resumes her work.

                    BARBIE MARGOT
          Who... who are you?

We hear the Executives in the hallway, yelling, trying
doorknobs. Barbie Margot tenses. Without looking up, the
older woman indicates a closet next to the refrigerator.

                    1950 WOMAN
          If you go through that closet,
          you'll find a stairwell down to the
          lobby. Just be careful of the mops
          and brooms.

                    BARBIE MARGOT
          Thank you... ?

                    1950 WOMAN
                 (smiling)
          Ruth.

                    BARBIE MARGOT
          Thank you, Ruth.

                    RUTH
          You're welcome, Barbie.

Barbie Margot hesitates then enters the cupboard. She pushes
through the mops and brooms. The cupboard extends beyond and
Barbie Margot finds herself in a narrow back stairwell.

INT. LOBBY/EXT. STREET

Barbie Margot scampers across the lobby and onto the busy
street. She looks around desperately. She glances back
through the glass windows. Mattel Executives sliding across
the shiny, slippery lobby floor.

Barbie freezes, panicked. Gloria's car pulls up, door
opening.

                    GLORIA
          Get in!

Barbie Margot then SEES Gloria. Time slows down. It's the
"love look" completed. They see each other seeing each other.

Just then the Mattel Executives come running out of the
building.

                    GLORIA
          NOW! GET IN *NOW*!

Barbie Margot leaps into the back seat. The door slams shut
and the car screeches off.

Town cars and vans pull up. The executives scramble inside.

                    MATTEL CEO
          Follow that Barbie!

INT. GLORIA'S CAR.

Gloria drives, making crazy turns. She's an *incredible*
driver. Sasha in the passenger seat. Everyone is screaming.

                    SASHA
              (*so* embarrassed)
          God I hope nobody from school saw
          us put a life-size Barbie in our
          car. How did this even *happen?!*

Mattel gains on them. Gloria does some *crazy amazing* driving.

                    GLORIA
          I don't know!

                    SASHA
          How are you here? You're like, an
          idea.

                    BARBIE MARGOT
          A GREAT idea.

                    GLORIA
          So, I've been a little lonely
          lately and I found the Barbies we
          used play with --

          SASHA   GLORIA
I thought we gave those away!   And I started playing and
                                 making drawings like we used
                                 to do together because I
                                 thought it would be fun and
                                 joyful--

                    BARBIE MARGOT
               (she understands)
          But it wasn't, was it?

                    GLORIA
          No, because I started feeling sad
          and weird and then the drawings got
          sad and weird... and maybe because
          I couldn't be like you I ended up
          making you like me?

                    BARBIE MARGOT
          Did any of these drawings by chance
          have thoughts of death and
          cellulite?

                    GLORIA
          YES! IRREPRESSIBLE THOUGHTS OF
          DEATH BARBIE!

                    BARBIE MARGOT
          OH MY GOD!

                    GLORIA
          And CELLULITE!

          BARBIE MARGOT   GLORIA
I came for YOU!   YOU came for ME!

                    SASHA
          What?!

                    BARBIE MARGOT
          Those were YOUR memories!

CUT BACK to earlier images of mother and daughter, but this time we see *Gloria's experience*, the joy of participating in Sasha's childhood and the pain of Sasha inevitably moving away as she grows up.

BACK to THE CAR:

> SASHA
> What? Are you two, like, Shining???

> GLORIA
> No, it's nothing like THAT!

> SASHA
> Are you Shining with a REAL Barbie?

> GLORIA
> No! Well, I mean, kind of... YES!

Gloria makes a crazy, screeching turn. (This should feel like the chase in Bullitt!)

> SASHA
> I don't even know where to start
> with this wishing a Barbie to life
> crap.

> GLORIA
> Listen, I'm just a boring Mom with
> a boring job and a daughter who
> hates me. Can you blame me for
> wanting a little fun?

Gloria checks the rearview mirror. The Mattel cars flanking.

> GLORIA
> I'm going to have to lose these
> chuckleheads.

She makes another crazy turn: *clearly* Gloria is NOT boring.

> SASHA
> Mom!

Everyone slides over, Barbie Margot falling. Gloria rights the car, Barbie Margot climbs back up, her hair a mess.

> BARBIE MARGOT
> (shaking her head)
> I think I owe you ladies an
> apology. I thought Barbie had made
> the Real World better, but the Real
> World is forever and irrevocably
> messed up!

                         GLORIA
          Well the real world isn't *perfect,*
          but you inspired _ME_!

                         BARBIE MARGOT
                    (depressed)
          But I *love* women, I want to *help*
          women.

                         SASHA
          Oh, come off it, everybody hates
          women. Women hate women and men
          hate women. It's the thing we can
          all agree on.

                         BARBIE MARGOT
                    (horrified)
          Is that true?

          GLORIA   SASHA
It's complicated... hate is a   Wake up Mom!
strong word.

Two cars appear on either side. The Mattel executives
yelling, but we can't hear anything they're saying through
their tinted windows.

                         GLORIA
          I am WIDE awake Sasha!

Gloria turns the wheel smashing into the side of a median
strip, sending them skidding.

                         SASHA
          MOM! Where did you learn to drive
          like this?

                         GLORIA
          There was this guy...

                         SASHA
          Was it dad?

                         GLORIA
                    (vague)
          Yeah... yeah it was dad.

Gloria does a crazy reverse, Tokyo Drift thing right into a
hidden alley. Everyone quiets as the Mattel vans drive by,
not seeing them.

                         GLORIA
          I can't hold them off forever.

                    BARBIE MARGOT
                  (suddenly)
             WAIT! I have an idea! Can you get
             us to Venice Beach?!

EXT. VENICE BEACH. 20 MINUTES LATER

They roller blade, frantically.

                    GLORIA
             Where are we going?!

                    BARBIE MARGOT
             Barbie Land! We'll be safe there!

                    SASHA
             WHAT?! Mom, are you really going to
             let Barbie take you and your tween
             daughter to an imaginary land?

                    GLORIA
             Yes and you know why? Because I
             never get to do anything. I didn't
             even go on that cruise I won at
             your school raffle because I didn't
             have enough vacation days and your
             dad is allergic to sun.

                    SASHA
             What *about* Dad? We can't just leave
             him!

                    GLORIA
             He'll be fine.

CUT to Nerdy Well Meaning Dad, in sandals and socks, learning
Spanish from an app.

                    NERDY WELL MEANING DAD
                  (into his phone, loud)
             Boligrafos.

                    APP
             Muy bien!

BACK to our group.

                    SASHA
             Yeah, he'll be fine.

                    BARBIE MARGOT
             Ready for fun! Here we go!

TRANSPORTATION MONTAGE

AND: We replay *some* of the various vehicles.

First is **Snowmobile**. Cute winter wear!

>   SASHA
>   Where are we! How did we get into
>   these clothes?

>   BARBIE MARGOT
>   (a twinkle in her eye)
>   How did you get into this vehicle?

>   GLORIA
>   (looking down)
>   When I was a kid, I lost these
>   boots and my mom wouldn't let me
>   buy a whole new Barbie just to
>   replace the boots!

>   BARBIE MARGOT
>   They look so good on you.

>   GLORIA
>   Why thank you!

Sasha does an eye roll.

Camper. They're all chilling in lawn chairs.

>   GLORIA
>   (admiring Barbie Margot)
>   She was always my favorite Barbie.

>   BARBIE MARGOT
>   And *you* are my favorite human!

Tandem Bike. It's now a three seater!

>   GLORIA
>   Don't tell him, but I never got a
>   Ken.

>   BARBIE MARGOT
>   That's because Ken is totally
>   superfluous!

They all crack up - Barbie Margot and Gloria are real pals.

Rocket.

>   BARBIE MARGOT
>   Women hold all major positions of
>   power, control all the money,
>   basically everything men do in your
>   world, women do in ours.
>
>   SASHA
>   (bending a little)
>   I mean, that sounds kind of cool.

Boat. Sasha is laughing as they take the waves in the speed boat. The experience, as bizarre as it is, can't help but delight her. Sasha then regards her mother regarding her:

>   GLORIA
>   Look! Dolphins!

EXT. BARBIE LAND. BARBIE CAR. DAY

Barbie, Gloria and Sasha cruise in the Barbie Car. Indigo Girls "Closer to Fine" playing on the radio, as always

>   BARBIE MARGOT   GLORIA
>   (singing)   (also singing)
>   I went to the doctor / I went   I went to the doctor / I went
>   to the mountain.   to the mountain.
>
>   SASHA   BARBIE MARGOT
>   WHAT IS THIS SONG?!   (going on)
>   ... and we have a female
>   president!
>
>   BARBIE MARGOT
>   And it's fun and work and
>   friendship and female 24/7.
>
>   SASHA
>   Do giant hands come in and play
>   with you?
>
>   BARBIE MARGOT
>   What? No. That's *crazy*.

CUT BACK TO: VENICE BEACH. REAL WORLD

Mattel Executives talk to locals on the Boardwalk who tell them what they saw earlier.

>   MUSCULAR VENICE BEACH PERSON
>   (pointing indistinctly)
>   A blonde, a brunette and a tween
>   roller bladed in that direction...

                     MATTEL CEO
                   (ominous)
               The first step is always
               rollerblading.

          AARON DINKINS   MATTEL CEO
        (he's tagged along)   They've gone to Barbie Land.
    Excuse me, sir?

                     AARON DINKINS
               Oh no.

                     MATTEL CEO
               And she brought humans there with
               her. This could mean extremely
               weird things for our world.

                     AARON DINKINS
               Like what?

                     MATTEL CEO
               Like nothing any of our collective
               imaginations COULD EVER DREAM UP.

    Aaron Dinkins looks peculiar, trying to imagine.

                     EXECUTIVE #1
               A podcast hosted by two wise trees?
               Or a choir of two thousand young
               fathers...

                     MATTEL CEO
               Not even CLOSE.
                   (to the others)
               We've got to get to Barbie Land!
               GO! Find some blades. Just pick a
               direction and run!

    They scatter.

    EXT. BARBIE LAND. DAY.

    Gloria and Sasha are totally impressed by the beauty of
    BARBIE LAND as they drive by the ocean in Barbie's
    convertible.

                     BARBIE MARGOT
                   (soaking it all in)
               I can feel my heels lifting
               already. Yes, this is what I was
               supposed to do. Bring you back
               here!

                    GLORIA
                 (so happy)
          It feels right!

                    BARBIE MARGOT
             It does!

They pass the BEACH. Kens are playing volleyball a la Top Gun
and the Barbies are cheering (reverse of beginning).

                    BARBIE MARGOT
             That's strange...

Also Kens race on the beach and hug triumphantly in the surf
(a la Rocky III). Barbie Issa hands a Ken a beer.

                    BARBIE ISSA
             Incoming brewski beer--
                 (she makes plane sounds)

                    BARBIE MARGOT
             Uh, so that's our president with
             the beer. And the cheering squad...
             is the supreme court?

                    BARBIE ISSA
             This is so much better than being
             President!!

                    BARBIE MARGOT
             Something's weird today.

A Ken Mermaid leaps out of the surf and waves. You don't
think that's a thing? Check this out:

                    KEN MERMAID
             Hi Barbie!

                    BARBIE MARGOT
                 (slightly taken aback))
             Oh... OK. Hi Ken.

Barbie Mermaid emerges and hands the Ken Mermaid a beer.

                    BARBIE MERMAID
          Here have a brewski beer! My big
          guy is thirsty!

                    BARBIE MARGOT
          Huh.
               (shaking it off)
          OK. Wait until you see my
          Dreamhouse. Everything I've bought
          and owned will totally inspire you.
          We'll change clothes again!

They pass the Capitol.

                    BARBIE MARGOT
          And that's the Capitol!

                    SASHA
          It's pink!!

And finally they pass Barbie Mt. Rushmore, but now instead of
Barbies it's... horses?!

                    BARBIE MARGOT
               (frowns)
          Huh.

EXT. BARBIE MARGOT'S DREAMHOUSE

They drive through the neighborhood.

                    BARBIE MARGOT
          And these are the Dreamhouses! This
          is where I live.

As they arrive in the cul-de-sac, Gloria exclaims.

                    GLORIA
               (still in awe)
          You can see through the houses!

                    SASHA
          So each Barbie has their own house?
          Where do the Kens stay?

                    BARBIE MARGOT
               (this has never occurred
                to her before)
          I don't know!

                         GLORIA
                    (nerding out)
               I had that treehouse! I saved up my
               allowance to buy it.

A Ken sits on the swing and waves to them. Barbie cocks her
head. Strange.

They pass a giant Hummer with flames--

                         BARBIE MARGOT
               I've never seen a car like that
               before... what happened here?

She finally takes in the full transformation - There are mini-
fridges everywhere, that poster of dogs playing poker, video
games, BIG TVs playing horse footage, Doritos, Mini
basketball hoops & arcade games, chin-up bars in the
doorways, foosball, pool, ping pong, air hockey, it's all Ken
all the time, empowered through some strange game of
telephone with the real world...

Some of them have beards, some mustaches, a couple have
goatees. Every Ken is there, including Ken Simu. This embrace
of a Real World cartoon masculinity seems to have united
them. A now bearded Ken Ryan Gosling sporting a mink coat is
in the middle of a monologue. All the Kens listen, rapt.

                         KEN RYAN GOSLING
                    (rotating through all the
                    man-activities)
               At first I thought the Real World
               was run by men, and then for one
               minute I thought it was run by
               horses, but now I realize that
               horses are just men-extenders. So
               are cars, buildings, airplanes,
               EVERYTHING! Everything exists just
               to expand and elevate the presence
               of MEN!

                         KEN KINGSLEY
               That's _amazing_!

                         BARBIE MARGOT (O.S.)
               Ken, what have you done?! What are
               you wearing?!

The Kens turn to see Barbie Margot, Gloria and Sasha. Ken
Ryan Gosling is secretly _thrilled_ she showed up. He'd been
wanting her to see what he was capable of. He tries to cover
with nonchalance.

                    KEN RYAN GOSLING
          Don't question it. Just roll with
          it tiny baby.

                    BARBIE MARGOT
          Don't call me "baby!"

He's hurt, but instead of admitting it, now he's going to go
full-out aggressive and posturing.

                    KEN RYAN GOSLING
          Ok, what about Mini Baby like this
          mini-fridge?

Ken Ryan Gosling opens the door to his mini-fridge and grabs
a beer. Laughter from the Kens. Allan sits with the Kens on a
leather couch and looks miserable.

                    BARBIE MARGOT
          This is MY Dreamhouse.

                    KEN RYAN GOSLING
          This is no longer "Barbie's
          Dreamhouse," this shall henceforth
          be known as "Ken's Mojo Dojo Casa
          House."

                    SASHA
          You don't have to say "Dojo" and
          "House."

                    GLORIA
          And "Casa."

                    KEN RYAN GOSLING
          But ya do. Because it feels so
          good. Try it. Mojo. Dojo. Casa.
          House.

Gloria and Sasha begin to repeat it back to Ken Ryan Gosling.
Barbie Margot shushes them to stop as Ken laughs maniacally.

EXT/INT. MATTEL SHIPPING WAREHOUSE. REAL WORLD. DAY

People loading Ken Mojo Dojo Casa Houses onto forklifts.

                    MATTEL CEO (O.S.)
               (yelling into his phone)
          Give it to me straight - how weird
          is it?

                    WAREHOUSE EMPLOYEE
          These Mojo Dojo Casa Houses are
          literally flying off the shelves!
                    (MORE)

>   WAREHOUSE EMPLOYEE (CONT'D)
> The kids are CLAMORING for them!
> Ken is on t-shirts, mugs, it's the
> number one tattoo. Warner Bros has
> started auditions for the Ken
> movie. Which is already a
> blockbuster hit!

EXT. VENICE BEACH. REAL WORLD. DAY

All the Mattel execs are roller blading. The CEO reacting to
the news on his phone.

>   MATTEL CEO   AARON DINKINS
> It's happening. That thing we   - Executive Assistant -
> could never imagine. If we
> don't get my Words Lady -

>   MATTEL CEO
> Executive Words Lady and someone
> who is probably her daughter back
> here and close the portal, our
> world could be altered forever.

>   EXECUTIVE #2
> But what does it matter if it's
> Barbie or Ken? The money is pouring
> in!

>   MATTEL CEO
> Shame on you, Executive Number 2!
> Do you think I spent my entire life
> in board rooms because of a bottom
> line?!

They all look away not wanting to answer this.

>   MATTEL CEO
> No! I got into this business
> because of little girls and their
> dreams! In the least creepy way
> possible!
>   (back to panic)
> BLADE FASTER! Time is running out!

EXT. BARBIE MARGOT'S DREAMHOUSE

Ken Ryan Gosling swings a golf club through some plastic
flowers in the yard. Barbie Margot reacts.

>   KEN RYAN GOSLING
> Look, I'm just hanging down with my
> bro-homies having a brewski beer in
> my Mojo Dojo Casa House.
>   (to Barbie Margot)
>   (MORE)

                    KEN RYAN GOSLING (CONT'D)
You can stay here if you want as my
bride-wife or my long-term-low-
commitment-distance girlfriend.
Now, brewski beer me.

                    BARBIE MARGOT
I will NOT brewski beer you.

                    KEN RYAN GOSLING
That's fine. I mean, without you
Barbies running things, we can do
our hair however we like--

We see Kens with crazy patches of beard on their faces.

                    KEN KINGSLEY
I have hats.

Barbie Emma enters in a French Maid outfit, Barbie Hari in a
Naughty Schoolgirl outfit.

                    BARBIE EMMA
                  (brainwashed)
How are my hungry boys! Who wants
snacks?

                    BARBIE MARGOT
Barbie, I'm so glad to see you! Can
you believe what's happening?!

                    BARBIE EMMA
                  (body snatched)
I know! Isn't it great?

                    BARBIE HARI
                  (to the men)
Does anyone need a brewski-beer?

                    BARBIE MARGOT
What are you doing? You're a
doctor!

                    BARBIE HARI
Being a doctor was stressful and a
lot of work. I'm happy being
helpful decoration.

                    BARBIE EMMA
And Allan likes to help me give the
Kens foot-massages.

                    ALLAN
No, I don't. I don't like that.

Allan looks totally freaked out by what's happening. Barbie Sharon and Barbie Ana sit on a leather couch rubbing a Ken's feet.

>   BARBIES
>   We do!

>   KEN RYAN GOSLING
>   I'm so blotto-faced day-drunk.

Kens cheer in agreement.

>   KEN KINGSLEY
>   Ditto same-same that!

>   BARBIE EMMA
>   I like not having to make any
>   decisions. It's like a spa day for
>   my brain, forever.

>   BARBIE MARGOT
>   What's _wrong_ with her?!

>   KEN RYAN GOSLING
>   Nothing. We just explained the
>   impeccable immaculate seamless
>   garment of logic that is Patriarchy
>   and she crumbled.

>   GLORIA
>   (figuring it out)
>   Oh my God. It's like in the 1500s
>   with the indigenous people and
>   small pox. They had no defenses
>   against it.

>   KEN RYAN GOSLING
>   (no idea what she's
>   talking about)
>   Yeah!!

Ken Ryan Gosling climbs up onto the roof of his Hummer.

>   KEN RYAN GOSLING
>   Buckle up, babe, because Barbie
>   Land is now Ken Land and it'll be
>   just like Century City in Los
>   Angeles. Because they have it
>   figured out in Century City.
>   (describing a delicacy)
>   The minute you get out of your car,
>   you're like I can't believe how
>   great this place is.

Ken Simu nods vigorously. He LOVES it!

                    BARBIE MARGOT
          No! They don't. They don't have it
          figured out in Century City.
          Because we failed them.

With sudden, personal intensity, almost crying, based on a
life-time of feeling like a second class citizen:

                    KEN RYAN GOSLING
          No, *you* failed *me*! Out there I was
          a SOMEBODY! I walked down the
          street and people respected me just
          for WHO I AM.
               (to the Kens)
          One lady even asked me for the
          time.

                    KEN SIMU
          NO WAY!

                    KEN RYAN GOSLING
          WAY! Except for these dumb
          technicalities like MBAs and
          medical degrees and, I don't know,
          swim lessons, I could have ruled
          THAT world.

He attempts to slide down the hood of the Hummer but his mink
sticks to the metal and he moves at a glacial pace. Finally
landing on the ground:

                    KEN RYAN GOSLING
          But here I don't need any of those
          things. Here I'm just a DUDE! AND
          THAT IS ENOUGH!

He raises a remote with a sense of triumph and switches the
channel on giant gross TV that has, until this point, been
playing romantic horse footage.

                    BARBIE RITU (O.S.)
               (brainwashed)
          This has been such an *exciting* day!

EXT. CAPITOL STEPS. ON THE TV. DAY

A Newswoman (Barbie Ritu) interviews Ken Scott.

                    KEN SCOTT
          It sure has! And please call me Mr.
          Ken President Prime Minister Man.

                    BARBIE RITU
          Let's recap all the amazing changes
          and innovations thanks to the Kens!

CUT TO: THEATRE

Nobel prize ceremony. All the contestants are Kens and all
the judges are Ken.

                    ANNOUNCER
          The Nobel Prize in Horses goes to
          "KEN!"

It's Ken Ryan Gosling. He winks as he accepts his prize.

INT. ~~BARBIE~~ KEN OVAL OFFICE. DAY

Ken Scott, who is president, signs a bill into law with all
of the Ken senators standing around him.

INT. SUPREME COURT. DAY

Ken Kingsley argues in front of the Ken Supreme Court. The
Gallery erupts into rapturous applause.

EXT. PINK HOUSE. DAY

                    BARBIE RITU
          And now you're making all of this
          permanent with a _special election_
          to change the constitution!

                    KEN SCOTT
              (taking the microphone)
          That's right, in 48 hours all the
          Kens will go to the polls and vote
          to change the constitution to a
          government for the Kens, of the
          Kens and by the Kens!

EXT. MOJO DOJO CASA HOUSE. SAME

Ken Ryan Gosling turns triumphantly to Barbie Margot, but
also kind of wanting her approval.

                    BARBIE MARGOT
          You can't do this. This is Barbie
          Land. The Barbies worked hard and
          dreamed hard to make it everything
          it is. You can't just UNDO it in a
          day!

                    KEN RYAN GOSLING
          Literally and figuratively watch
          me.
               (echoing Barbie from
                earlier in the movie)
          Now, if you'll excuse me. This is
          MY Mojo Dojo Casa House. Not
          Barbie's Mojo Dojo Casa House.
          Right?

Barbie Margot looks devastated.

                    KEN RYAN GOSLING
               (quiet and sincere)
          See how it feels? It's not fun, is
          it?

                    ALL THE KENS
          It's boy's night!

A catch in his throat, this almost hurts him to say:

                    KEN RYAN GOSLING
          Every night is boy's night.

Ken Ryan Gosling feels for her, but then puts on sunglasses
to hide his emotion. Then he puts sunglasses on top of his
sunglasses and walks away. Cold as ice.

EXT. CUL-DE-SAC. DAY

Barbie Margot runs from the house *screaming*. Gloria and Sasha
follow. As she reaches the lawn, clothes and accessories come
raining down. Ken is tossing all her stuff off the third
floor.

                    KEN RYAN GOSLING
          And take your lady fashions with
          you!

He identifies each clothing set as it flies through the air.

                    KEN RYAN GOSLING
          Take your "Celebrate Disco" bell
          bottoms, take your "Ice Capades
          Pretty Practice Suit and Dazzling
          Show Skirt"...

Gloria surreptitiously picks up a few great pieces.

                    GLORIA
          These are *archival*!

                    KEN RYAN GOSLING
          ...your "Pajama Jam in Amsterdam"
          set AND your "Pretty Paisley
          Palazzo Pants" and get OUT.

He is angry but he still loves all the clothes and
obsessively calls them by their proper names, of course.

                    BARBIE MARGOT
          NOT THE PALAZZOS!!!

Ken Ryan Gosling collapses in a pool of emotion. Barbie
Margot runs crying. Gloria and Sasha follow. Gloria tries to
comfort her. Barbie Margot turns on Gloria, angry:

                    BARBIE MARGOT
          Why did you wish me to your messed
          up world using your complicated
          human thoughts and feelings?!
          Barbie Land was perfect before and
          I was perfect before!

                    GLORIA
          I'm so sorry I wasn't trying to do
          anything--

Sasha steps in, defending Gloria, who is touched.

                    SASHA
          Don't apologize -- Don't blame my
          Mom. Maybe you wished us? Maybe
          it's your fault, Barbie.

                    BARBIE MARGOT
          I didn't wish anything! I've never
          wanted anything to change.

                    GLORIA
          Well, honey, that's life. It's all
          change.

                    BARBIE MARGOT
          Well that's just terrifying. I
          don't want that. Not MY life. I'm
          just going sit here and wait and
          hope that one of the more
          leadership oriented Barbies snaps
          out of it and does something about
          this whole mess.

Barbie Margot drops listlessly into a sitting position, tips
over and lies flat like a doll.

GLORIA
I really understand this
feeling. It's basically like
being a human person all the
time--

BARBIE MARGOT
JUST LEAVE ME HERE! Go back
to your messed up world and
leave me to mine.

SASHA
So you're just going to give up? I
almost felt bad for you, but you
are exactly what I thought you
were.

GLORIA
Come on, honey, let's go

SASHA
How do we even--

BARBIE MARGOT
Do everything we did,
reversed.

Gloria and Sasha walk away.

SASHA
She doesn't deserve you.

Barbie Margot is now actually face down on the lawn.

BARBIE MARGOT
This is the lowest I've ever been.
Emotionally AND physically.

CUT TO:

A COMMERCIAL ON TV. It's all bright and happy except for the
dolls are really going through it. They look wrecked and sad.

ADVERTISING VOICE
Ok, kids! It's time to run out and
get the NEW Depression Barbie! She
wears sweatpants all day and night,
she spent seven hours today on
Instagram looking at her estranged
best friend's engagement photos
while eating a family sized bag of
Starbursts and now her jaw is
KILLING her and she's going to
watch the BBC's Pride and Prejudice
for the seventh time until she
falls asleep. (Anxiety, panic
attacks and OCD sold separately).

EXT. ~~BARBIE~~ KEN LAND STREET. DAY.

Weird Barbie patrols in a vehicle version of her house,
constructed from abandoned Barbie cars. It's kind of like a
tank, very Road Warrior.

It rumbles past a Ken taking down "Barbie Way" and putting up
a "Ken Avenue Boulevard Road Mews" sign. They screech to a
halt beside a catatonic Barbie Margot:

>   WEIRD BARBIE
>   Got a live one here!

Earring Magic Ken and Barbie Video Girl pick Barbie Margot
up. From Barbie Margot's point of view we see Weird Barbie.

>   BARBIE MARGOT
>   I'm like you now. Ugly and
>   unwanted.

>   WEIRD BARBIE
>   Thanks, kid.

Barbie Margot is lifted into the amazing, cock-eyed vehicle.

EXT. TRANSPORTATION MONTAGE

TANDEM BIKE. With the CEO at the front and Aaron Dinkens in
the back, Mattel rides a 12 person tandem bike on their
journey to Barbie Land!

>   MATTEL CEO
>   (shouting to the group)
>   Isn't this great!! Wait until you
>   see the boat!

INT/EXT. BARBIE CAR. OPEN ROAD.

Gloria and Sasha are driving down the Barbie highway in
Barbie's car. Gloria and Sasha (!!!) sing at the top of their
lungs to the Indigo Girls.

>   GLORIA AND SASHA
>   "I went to the doctor / I went to
>   the mountains / I looked to the
>   children / I drank from the
>   fountains..."

Sasha looks almost *wistfully* at the retreating landscape of
Barbie Land.

Suddenly the song on the radio is cut out by a needle
scratch. Gloria frowns. A Ken comes over the airwaves.

                KEN RADIO DJ
        We interrupt this broadcast to
        bring you our NEW radio station
        KKEN 107.5. Playing Ken's favorite
        song over and over again!

And then suddenly Matchbox 20's "Push" erupts from the
speakers. Allan pops up in the backseat:

                ALLAN
      TURN THIS SONG OFF FOR CHRISTSAKE!

Gloria and Sasha scream their heads off and Allan screams at
their screaming. So much screaming! They skid off the road,
crashing down a hill, flipping over a few times and landing
upright on another road. (SAME SHOT AS THE FIRST TIME.)
Except for this time, the car lands with no one in it, and
ONE second later, right beside the car, in the same
configuration, land Gloria, Sasha, & Allan.

              MATCHBOX 20
          (singing)
        "I want to push you around. Well, I
        will, well, I will..."

Still hysterical, getting to their feet:

                SASHA
        Who are *you*?!

                ALLAN
        I'm Allan!

                GLORIA
        You *ARE* Allan. That's great!

                ALLAN
        Don't tell the Kens, I'm trying to
        escape. I cannot sit on ONE MORE
        LEATHER COUCH. It's gonna break my
        SPIRIT.

Up ahead the Kens are building a wall. It's partially
constructed, and hard hat Kens hammer and dig.

                ALLAN
        Once they figure out how to build
        that wall sideways and not just up,
        no one will be able to get in or
        out.

It's true: they're building the wall STRAIGHT up, not across.

                    ALLAN
          If we want to leave we better make
          a run for it.

                    GLORIA
          Allan, you can't go. Having a
          Barbie in the real world is what
          caused all these problems in the
          first place.

                    ALLAN
          Not *one person* would care if Allan
          was in the real world. In fact it's
          happened before...
                    (a secret)
          All of NSYNC... Allan.

Off their looks--

                    ALLAN
          Yes, even him. So... COME ON!

                    KEN CONSTRUCTION WORKER
          Hey, you there!

Allan casually stands and walks towards the Kens.

                    ALLAN
                    (to Gloria and Sasha)
          Just get in the car and keep it
          singing... be ready for anything.
                    (to the Ken)
          Hey man!

                    KEN CONSTRUCTION WORKER
          Who are you?

                    ALLAN
          I'm Allan, I'm Ken's buddy? All his
          clothes fit me!!

Allan charges at the Kens and takes them all on, rather
impressively. Gloria and Sasha scramble to the car. Sasha
lands in the driver's seat and REVS:

                    GLORIA
          You don't have a driver's license!

                    SASHA
          And this car doesn't have an
          engine!

Sasha looks beyond the wall and back to the Real World - and
then in the other direction, back to Barbie Land.

                    GLORIA
          What are you doing?! Let's GO!

Sasha looks at Gloria. And then, inspired:

                    SASHA
          We have to go back. Barbie Land
          needs saving. *Barbie* needs saving.

                    GLORIA
          But you hate Barbie!

                    SASHA
          But you don't! You've *always*
          believed in what she could be.

                    GLORIA
          Well I was wrong. Barbie gave up.
          The Kens won.

                    SASHA
          Mom, you have to try! Even if you
          can't make it perfect you can make
          it better.

                    GLORIA
               (breaking)
          I can't make anything better! I'm
          the one who ruined Barbie Land with
          my stupid drawings in the first
          place.

                    SASHA
               (firm)
          They're not stupid! They're
          amazing...

                    GLORIA
               (tearing up)
          You like my drawings?

                    SASHA
          They're weird and dark and crazy.
          Everything you pretend not to be.

                    GLORIA
          I am... I am weird, dark and crazy.

Allan punches the last Ken and takes a threatening step
toward the remaining beleaguered Kens.

                    ALLAN
          You want some more Allan?!

And he turns and runs back to the car.

                    ALLAN
          We have to get out of here RIGHT
          NOW!

Gloria hesitates.

                    GLORIA
          Shut up Allan! We're going back.
          Let's go help my doll.

Gloria and Sasha beam at each other. Sasha steps on the gas,
turns the wheel and they swing back *toward* Barbie Land.

                    ALLAN
          I'll never get out of here.

                    SASHA
          Where can we find Barbie?

                    ALLAN
          There's only one place she'd be.

INT. WEIRD BARBIE'S WEIRDHOUSE. DAY

Barbie Margot has joined Weird Barbie and her motley crew -
the reject Barbies, Earring Magic Ken, Sugar Daddy Ken,
Growing up Skipper -- her boobs grow when she lifts her arm --
Teen Talk Barbie, Tanner the pooping Dog, Video Girl Barbie.

Barbie Margot is lying on the floor, unable to do anything,
totally without any will to live. Teen Talk Barbie and Video
Girl Barbie attempt to un-brainwash Barbie Alexandra.

                    TEEN TALK BARBIE
               (to Barbie Alexandra)
          You're a _writer_. This is your Nobel
          Prize. Remember?

Barbie Alexandra goes into one of those acceptance speeches
women give, totally self-effacing and not embracing the win.

                    BARBIE ALEXANDRA
          Oh my God, I don't even *know* how I
          got here. I don't deserve this! I'd
          like to thank Ken.

                    WEIRD BARBIE
               (entering the room)
          It's pointless trying to deprogram
          her. I've already tried.
               (looking at Barbie Margot)
                    (MORE)

                    WEIRD BARBIE (CONT'D)
The fork in my soup is this, Barb:
why didn't the brainwashing work on
you?

                    BARBIE MARGOT
              (still face down)
My exposure to Patriarchy in the
real world made me immune. Either
you're brainwashed or you're weird
and ugly. There is no in-between.

                    WEIRD BARBIE
Sing it sister.
              (to the group)
Get ready to live in the shadows
and on the margins because in 48
hours Barbie Land becomes Ken Land.

They hear voices. Everyone screams and then tries to hide,
badly. Except for Barbie Margot, who doesn't move. Other
Barbies step over her. Some try to freeze like statues.

                    WEIRD BARBIE
It's the Kens! They've found us!

The sound of footsteps grow louder. Until finally Gloria,
Sasha and Allan are standing there.

                    WEIRD BARBIE
       HUMANS!

                    ALLAN
AND **ALLAN**!

The lights go on and they all emerge out of their random
hiding places. Barbie Margot half clocks Gloria and Sasha and
tries to pull herself away, out of their sight.

                    WEIRD BARBIE
              (to Sasha and Gloria)
Welcome, welcome to my Weirdhouse -
I'm Weird Barbie. I'm in the
splits, have a funky hair cut and I
smell like basement.

                    GLORIA
OH MY GOD I HAD A WEIRD BARBIE!

                    WEIRD BARBIE
Yeah you did.

                    GLORIA
YOU MAKE THEM WEIRD BY PLAYING TOO
HARD!

Again, we take in the group as Gloria identifies each one --

                    GLORIA
          That's Sugar Daddy Ken! And Earring
          Magic Ken! Mattel discontinued
          them...

                    SASHA
          Sugar Daddy Ken? WTF?

                    SUGAR DADDY KEN
          No, no, I'm not a Sugar Daddy. This
          is Sugar.
                    (holding up a dog)
          And I'm her *Daddy*.

                    EARRING MAGIC KEN
          And I have an earring. A magic
          earring.

                    GLORIA
                    (to Sasha)
          Yeah, those were actual Kens.
                    (identifying all of them)
          And-- more discontinued Barbies!!
          Growing Up Skipper?! May I?
                    (to Sasha)
          Watch this!

Gloria lifts Growing Up Skipper's arm and her boobs inflate.
This is as weird as it sounds.

                    GLORIA
          See! Her boobs grow!

                    SASHA
                    (aghast)
          Why would they do that?

Gloria continues down the line of discontinued Barbies.

                    GLORIA
          And Barbie Video Girl!

                    BARBIE VIDEO GIRL
          I have a TV in my back. You know
          whose dream that is? Nobody. It's
          nobody's dream.

                    WEIRD BARBIE
          And that's Barbie Barbie, of
          course... she's not dead she's just
          having an existential crisis.

Gloria and Sasha walk over to Barbie Margot who hasn't gotten very far. She just presses her face to the ground.

Gloria turns her over. Barbie Margot hides her face with her hands. Gloria gently moves them away.

And there is unadorned Barbie Margot, no makeup, nothing special just her (which WE KNOW is INSANELY BEAUTIFUL, don't worry.) Barbie Margot totally falls apart weeping. Like a toddler crying.

                    GLORIA
          What's wrong?

                    BARBIE MARGOT
               (between sobs)
          I'm... not... pretty... any...
          more...

                    GLORIA
          What? You're SO pretty.

                    BARBIE MARGOT
               (shaking her head)
          Not "Stereotypical Barbie"
          pretty...

                    HELEN MIRREN (V.O.)
               (interrupting)
          Note to the filmmakers: You should
          have never cast Margot Robbie if
          you wanted to make this point.

                    GLORIA
          You are *beautiful*.

                    BARBIE MARGOT
          ... it's not just that... I'm not
          smart enough to be interesting...

                    GLORIA
          But you ARE smart.

                    BARBIE MARGOT
          I can't do brain surgery, I've
          never flown a plan, I'm not
          president, no one on the Supreme
          Court is me... I'm just... not...
          good... enough...for... anything
          ...

She sobs bitterly. Gloria shakes her head, feels deeply:

                         GLORIA
          IT IS LITERALLY IMPOSSIBLE TO BE A
          WOMAN! You are *so* beautiful and *so*
          smart and it *kills* me that you
          don't think you're good enough.
          Like we have to always be
          extraordinary and somehow we're
          always doing it wrong. You're
          supposed to be THIN but not TOO
          THIN and you can never say you want
          to be THIN you have to say you want
          to be HEALTHY but you also have to
          BE thin. You have to have money but
          you can't ask for money because
          that's crass. You have to be a boss
          but you can't be mean. You're
          supposed to lead but you can't
          squash other people's ideas. You're
          supposed to LOVE being a mother but
          don't talk about your kids all the
          damn time. You're supposed to be a
          career woman but always be looking
          out for other people. You have to
          answer for men's bad behavior,
          which is INSANE, but if you point
          that out then you're accused of
          complaining. You're supposed to be
          pretty for men but not SO pretty
          that you tempt them too much or
          threaten other women. You're
          supposed to be part of the
          sisterhood but also stand out but
          also always be grateful. You have
          to never get old never be rude
          never show off never be selfish
          never fall down never fail never
          show fear never get out of line.
          It's too hard, it's too
          contradictory and no one says thank
          you or gives you a medal, and in
          fact, it turns out, somehow, that
          not only are you doing it all wrong
          but that everything is also YOUR
          fault. I'm just so damn tired of
          watching myself and every single
          other women tie ourselves in knots
          so that people will like us. And if
          all that is also true for a <u>doll</u>
          just *representing* a woman then I
          don't even know!

Exhausted, she sits down. Allan is in tears, they all are.
Maybe a slow clap? And then:

                    BARBIE ALEXANDRA
          Wait, I did write a book.
                    (rubbing her eyes)
          It was like I was in some dream
          where I was somehow really invested
          in the Zack Snyder cut of Justice
          League.
                    (shaking her head, looking
                     to Gloria)
          But what you said - it broke me out
          of it.

                         GLORIA
          Really?!

                    WEIRD BARBIE
          She's back! You're back!

Sasha looks at her mom like she's seeing her for the first
time. She is proud.

Barbie Margot stands up. And we MOVE in on her pure, tear-
streaked face.

                    BARBIE MARGOT
          By giving voice to the cognitive
          dissonance required to be a woman
          under the patriarchy, you robbed it
          of it's power.

Gloria, Sasha and everyone else turns to Barbie Margot:

                    BARBIE MARGOT
                    (surprised and impressed)
          Woah, I just said all of that.

                         SASHA
          Hell yes, White Savior Barbie!

                    BARBIE MARGOT
          No, it was your Mom. She did the
          saving.

Sasha fist bumps her. Barbie Margot is amazed. She suddenly
has new authority, a deeper voice, from a place of real
knowing, like Olivia de Havilland at the end of "The
Heiress." (Now, go watch that movie!)

                    BARBIE MARGOT
          We have to stop the Kens.
                    (to Gloria)
          You've got to say those things to
          all the other Barbies. That's the
          key.

>   BARBIE ALEXANDRA
> How will we get them away from
> their Kens?

>   SASHA
> We have experience with a world
> like this one.

>   BARBIE MARGOT
>   (to Weird Barbie)
> Do you have a map of Barbie Land?

>   WEIRD BARBIE
>   (triumphantly)
> What do you think.

A large 3D map of Barbie Land opens up (like a Murphy bed) from the wall.

CUT TO: HEIST MONTAGE. We see the execution of the plan as Barbie Margot, Gloria and Sasha lay out the details. (You know that thing, you've seen it in every heist movie ever!)

>   BARBIE MARGOT
> Here's the deal. It's not just
> about how they see us, it's about
> how they see themselves.

>   GLORIA
> Ken Land contains the seeds of its
> own destruction.

>   BARBIE MARGOT
> First we have to get the Barbies
> away from their Kens. We can use a
> decoy Barbie who pretends to be
> brainwashed.
>   (to Barbie Alexandra)
> That should be you.

>   SASHA
> We'll distract them by pretending
> to be helpless and confused. Kens
> can't resist a damsel in distress.

>   GLORIA
> You have to make them believe that
> you're complacent and that they
> have the power. And when their
> guard is down you can take the
> power back.

CUT TO: The Barbie Busytown Street. The "heist Barbies" pile out of Weird Barbie's tank-car.

Barbie Alexandra sits in a cafe on her laptop. She nods to the "heist Barbies" as Ken Simu strolls by with Barbie Issa.

>   KEN SIMU
>   The influence that Porsche 356 has
>   had on the motoring world as a
>   whole cannot be overstated.

>   BARBIE ISSA
>   The 356! How could I be so
>   ignorant?!

>   BARBIE ALEXANDRA
>   (theatrically)
>   Ugh Photoshop is so hard! I just
>   don't understand how to use the
>   Select tool!

Ken Simu immediately leaves Barbie Issa's side for Barbie Alexandra.

>   KEN SIMU
>   Oh, honey, you can only use the
>   Select tool if the layer is
>   highlighted. Here, let me show
>   you...

He wraps his arms around her to use her keyboard.

>   BARBIE ALEXANDRA
>   Ugh my tiny head is just swimming
>   with technical jargon like color
>   bands and magnetic lassos...

>   BARBIE MARGOT (V.O.)
>   Once they're engaged, we'll spirit
>   away their Barbie and deprogram her-

We see Barbie Margot and Allan hurrying Barbie Issa away from the scene. She's thrown into the Weird Barbie tank-car and Gloria de-programs her:

>   GLORIA
>   (at Barbie Issa)
>   ... you're supposed to be their
>   mommies but not remind them of
>   their mommy, any power you have
>   must be masked under a giggle...

This snaps Barbie Issa out of her stupor.

>   BARBIE ISSA
>   (blinks)
>   What happened?
>   (MORE)

                    BARBIE ISSA (CONT'D)
          One day I was president, the next
          thing I know I was cutting a Ken's
          steak for him...?

                    GLORIA
          Welcome back, Madame President.

                    BARBIE MARGOT (V.O.)
          And then we'll recruit the now
          unbrainwashed Barbies to our cause.
          They can be the new decoys.

INTERCUT THE PLAN. The Barbies distract the Kens by
pretending to be helpless and then Gloria deprograms them.

                    GLORIA (V.O.)
          Tell him you've never seen the
          Godfather and you'd love him to
          explain it to you.

In a Ken Mojo Dojo Casa House, Ken Kingsley sits with Barbie
Sharon in front of one of the giant TVs talking over the
movie.

                    BARBIE ISSA
          Are you watching the God*father*?

                    KEN KINGSLEY
          It's the "Godfather."

                    BARBIE ISSA
          I've never seen it!

The now de-brainwashed Barbie Issa sits beside him, feigning
total interest.

                    KEN KINGSLEY
          Oh my god you've never seen The
          Godfather? The movie is a rich
          blend of Coppola's aesthetic genius
          and a triumph of Robert Evans and
          the architecture of the 70's studio
          system--

She nods and smiles and while he's busy blathering on about
the movie, Barbie Margot and Weird Barbie gently "kidnap"
Barbie Sharon, and lead her to Gloria who does another
version of her speech.

                    GLORIA
          You have to reject men's advances
          without damaging their egos,
          because if you say yes to them,
          you're a tramp, and if you say no
          to them, you're a prude.

Barbie Sharon blinks, awakened.

                    BARBIE SHARON
          I don't want to touch a foot.

                    GLORIA
          No, you don't.

                    SASHA (V.O.)
          Be confused about money.

Now it's Barbie Sharon helping! She sits with a a bunch of
financial documents.

                    BARBIE SHARON
          Oh, I just have all my money in a
          Savings account--

                    KEN SCOTT
             (opening a briefcase)
          That's totally wrong. You need
          treasury bonds, corporate bonds.
          CDs.

                    BARBIE SHARON
          No one has CDs anymore!

                    KEN SCOTT
          Oh sweetheart you are just so cute
          when you're confused. But no, not
          music CDs, CD stands for
          Certificate of Deposit which is
          issued by the bank to...

They steal away HIS Barbie (Barbie Emma, in her maid outfit)
and deprogram her.

                    BARBIE EMMA
          What am I wearing?

And now Barbie Emma browses through albums while Ken Ncuti
puts on a record, with Barbie Ana by his side.

                    BARBIE EMMA
          I know what I like, but I don't
          know albums--

                    KEN NCUTI
               (abandoning Barbie Ana)
          Oh, my God, you've never heard of
          Pavement?!

                    BARBIE EMMA
          It's got a pretty cover--

                    KEN NCUTI
          Stephen Malkmus really harnessed
          the acerbic talk singing of Lou
          Reed with post punk influences such
          as Wire and The Fall.

                    GLORIA (V.O.)
          And then there are some classics of
          the trade.

Barbie Ana pretends she's drowning, by just lying down by the
side of the ocean. A Ken leans down to rescue her.

                    BARBIE ANA
               (batting her eyelashes)
          You might have to give me mouth to
          mouth.

And again the liberated Barbies steal away Barbie Hari.
Gloria ranting. Barbie Hari snapping out of it:

Then she executes the classic glasses gag:

                    BARBIE HARI
          Gee I am so awkward and don't feel
          pretty at all and will anyone ever
          like me?

                    KEN RYAN GOSLING
          May I...?

He takes off her glasses for her.

                    KEN RYAN GOSLING
          There! Now I can see your beautiful
          face!

                    GLORIA (V.O.)
          And then there's pretending to be
          terrible at every sport, ever.

CUT TO: Helpful Sports Montage! Barbie Sharon pretends to not
be able to hit a golf ball. Ken Scott approaches, wraps his
arms around her:

                    KEN SCOTT
          Here let me show you--

Barbie Alexandra tennis swing. Ken Kingsley arm wrap.

                    KEN KINGSLEY
          Here let me show you--

Barbie Hari baseball swing. Ken Simu arm wrap.

                    KEN SIMU
          Here let me show you--

Barbie Ana pulls the arrow back. Ken Ncuti arm wrap.

                    KEN NCUTI
          Here let me show you --

All the Kens at once, maybe in a "Team Photo" type thing:

                    KENS
          Here let us show you!

                    BARBIE MARGOT (V.O.)
          We'll do this until every single
          Barbie is deprogrammed and ready to
          take back Barbie Land.

INT. WEIRD BARBIE'S WEIRDHOUSE

The place is now bustling with Barbies who are back to
themselves. It's alive with chatter and planning. Weird
Barbie does a taxi whistle to get their attention.

                    WEIRD BARBIE
               (to the room)
          Tomorrow the Kens are going to vote
          to change the constitution but we
          have to get there first.

                    SASHA
          The final stage of our plan: To
          turn the Kens against each other.
          Now that they think they have power
          over _you_, you make them question
          whether they have enough power over
          each other.

CLOSE on Barbie Margot. A hand applies make-up to her face.
It's Gloria.

                    BARBIE MARGOT
          What if this doesn't work? What if
          he doesn't... like me anymore?

                        GLORIA
          He likes you...

                     BARBIE MARGOT
          But he was really upset...

                        GLORIA
          Because he likes you. And deep down
          he knows you don't feel the same
          way.

                     BARBIE MARGOT
          I still don't want to hurt him.

                        GLORIA
          He took your house. He brainwashed
          your friends. He wants to control
          the government...

                     BARBIE MARGOT
          Ok true. Right.
             (laughs)
          It's like I'm a woman already...

                        GLORIA
          Welcome.

                     BARBIE MARGOT
          Is this what it's really like?

They share a rueful smile as Gloria finishes.

Barbie Margot walks into the room of Barbies. They all smile
at her. She's "Stereotypical Barbie Perfect" again.

                     BARBIE MARGOT
          I'm ready. Here we go!

EXT. KEN'S MOJO DOJO CASA HOUSE

Barbie rings the bell. Ken Ryan Gosling sees her, pretends he
doesn't, noisily prepares himself, and then fakes being
shocked to see her. It's a lot.

                   KEN RYAN GOSLING
          Oh... hey. You've caught me
          reading.

                     BARBIE MARGOT
          Hey. I've been thinking.

                   KEN RYAN GOSLING
          Uh huh.

BARBIE MARGOT	KEN RYAN GOSLING
Ken Land is--	Kendom--

BARBIE MARGOT	KEN RYAN GOSLING
Kendom-	Kendom Land--

BARBIE MARGOT	KEN RYAN GOSLING
Land of--	The Free and Men--

                    BARBIE MARGOT
          Right. Well, this *place*--

                    KEN RYAN GOSLING
          Uh huh--

                    BARBIE MARGOT
          Is really great. I've never seen
          the Barbies so happy--

                    KEN RYAN GOSLING
          They've done a great job cheering.

                    BARBIE MARGOT
          Yeah, and the Kens really are
          better at ruling than the Barbies
          are--

                    KEN RYAN GOSLING
               (like it's nothing)
          We just took Patriarchy and made it
          Patriarchy.

BARBIE MARGOT	KEN RYAN GOSLING
(confused but moving along)	Yes?
Right and--	

                    BARBIE MARGOT
          And... I'm ready to be your long-
          term-distance-low-commitment-casual
          girlfriend if you'll still have me?

                    KEN RYAN GOSLING
               (clearly into this idea)
          Um... will you just hold on for one
          second.

Ken Ryan Gosling retreats into his house and out of view.

                    KEN RYAN GOSLING (O.S.)
          SUBLIME!

Returning to Barbie.

                    KEN RYAN GOSLING
          I don't know. I'm going to have to
          think about it.

                    BARBIE MARGOT
          Please?

                    KEN RYAN GOSLING
          Fine. Come inside and I can play
          the guitar at you.

                    BARBIE MARGOT
          Yay!

She hops inside.

INT. KEN'S MOJO DOJO CASA HOUSE

Ken Ryan Gosling plays guitar on the couch while staring at
Barbie Margot who listens patiently.

                    KEN RYAN GOSLING
                (to Barbie Margot)
          "I want to Push you down, well I
          will well I will."

EXT. BARBIE LAND. BEACH. NIGHT

4 Hours Later and he's still going. Now on the dunes. It's a
beach party with all the Kens and their Barbies. All the
Barbies pretend to be brainwashed, and all the Kens play
guitar at them. Yes, it's like 20 guitars. And one drum set.

                    KENS
                (to Barbies)
          "I want to Push you down, well I
          will well I will."

                    BARBIE MARGOT (V.O.)
          This is the final stage of our
          plan. Give them their dream come
          true...

                    GLORIA (V.O.)
          And at the peak of their happiness,
          when they think you actually care
          about this song...

                    SASHA (V.O.)
          You take it all away.

Margot looks across to Barbie Alexandra, who nods - it's
time. Then Barbie Margot looks at her phone and giggles.

                    KEN RYAN GOSLING
                  (immediately insecure)
             Who... who are you texting?

                    BARBIE MARGOT
                  (feigning innocence)
             Huh?

                    KEN RYAN GOSLING
             Who are you texting?

Anyone who asks that question twice has already lost all
power.

                    BARBIE MARGOT
             No one.

He snatches the phone.

                    KEN RYAN GOSLING
                  (reading)
             Ken!

                    BARBIE MARGOT
             Sorry, one sec...

We follow Barbie Margot and move throughout the Barbie/Ken
couples at the party, all playing their guitars at their
Barbies.

Barbie Margot approaches Ken Simu who also plays guitar and
sings Matchbox 20 at Barbie Alexandra.

                    BARBIE MARGOT
             That's a beautiful song you're
             playing. Did you write it?

                    KEN SIMU
             Yes. Want to sit here and watch me
             do it while staring into your eyes
             uncomfortably for four and a half
             minutes?

                    BARBIE MARGOT
             I'd love to.

Ken Ryan Gosling observes this, enraged. He smashes his
guitar into the sand but it doesn't break.

And now the other Barbies do similar things, walking across
the sand from their Kens to engage with opposing Kens.

                         BARBIE MARGOT (V.O.)
                You play on their egos and their
                petty jealousies and you turn them
                against each other. While they're
                fighting, we take back Barbie Land.

The Kens look at each other suspiciously. No Ken can be
trusted!

EXT/INT. KEN'S MOJO DOJO CASA HOUSES, CUL-DE-SAC. LATER

Ken Ryan Gosling, Ken Kingsley and Ken Ncuti sit on the edges
of their houses with their feet dangling. Because the houses
are open to the world, they can all see and talk to each
other. It's all very kid-like.

                         KEN NCUTI
                    (from his house)
                Does the title of long term-
                distance-low-commitment-casual
                girlfriend mean NOTHING?!

                         KEN RYAN GOSLING
                    (from his house)
                This has gone too far!

                         KEN NCUTI
                What do we do?!

                         KEN KINGSLEY
                    (from his house)
                We beach every individual one of
                them OFF!

                         KEN RYAN GOSLING
                No. We go to war!

                         KEN KINGSLEY
                Against the Barbies?

                         KEN RYAN GOSLING
                Against the Kens.

                         KEN KINGSLEY
                But we *are* the Kens.

                         KEN RYAN GOSLING
                The *other* Kens.

                         KEN KINGSLEY
                Well we should probably call them
                something else so it doesn't get
                confusing.

KEN RYAN GOSLING
No, we'll know what we mean.

KEN KINGSLEY
When we're on the battlefield and
you say, "Ken at four o'clock!" I
won't know if you mean us Kens or
the other Kens.

KEN RYAN GOSLING
Because, my dudes, we attack at 10
o'clock, to take advantage of the
morning waves.

KEN NCUTI
But not so early so we all get to
sleep in.

KEN RYAN GOSLING
Right.

KEN KINGSLEY
What will we fight with? We have no
guns.

KEN RYAN GOSLING
Tennis racquets and volley balls.

KEN NCUTI
And slap fights!

KEN RYAN GOSLING
And beach offs!

INT./EXT. MOJO DOJO CASA HOUSE. DAWN

In his bed, Ken Ryan Gosling is already awake, singing.

Then he and the other Kens mink up and walk towards battle,
Ryan still singing. Think "The Warriors."

The song continues as...

EXT. BARBIE LAND. BEACH. DAWN

They come in on paddle boats, Ken Ryan Gosling and Ken
Kingsley leading the charge, paddling furiously, trying to
look dignified in their arm floaties.

The other Kens, led by Ken Simu, are waiting on the dunes
mounted on hobby-horses.

                    KEN RYAN GOSLING
                 (unhinged screaming)
            I'll see you on the Malibu beach!

As they rush the beach in their trunks, they're also hitting
volleyballs and making sand castles. Maybe a game of Kadima?

                    KEN KINGSLEY
            The water is cold!

Slo-mo sand being kicked in Ken's faces.

EXT. ROOF OF WEIRD BARBIE'S. MORNING

All the Barbies, Barbie Margot, Weird Barbie, Gloria, Sasha,
and the rejected Barbies and Kens look over Barbie Land.

                    GLORIA
            And now they destroy themselves.

                    WEIRD BARBIE
            Should we go restore our
            constitution?

                    BARBIE EMMA
            Good idea.

EXT. BARBIE LAND. BEACH

BACK TO THE BEACH. The executives from Mattel in their suits
appear amidst the Kens on the beach.

                    MATTEL CEO
            This is a real hornet's nest in
            here.

Aaron Dinkins is hit in the head with a volleyball.

                    AARON DINKINS
            Ow!

Mattel Executive #1 laughs and then is suddenly and violently
shot in the arm in a real Saving Private Ryan way. He
crumples on the sand. Everyone looks at each other.

                    MATTEL EXECUTIVE #1
            Did I get shot? Are there real
            weapons here?

                    MATTEL CEO
                 (not convincing)
            No?

EXT. BARBIE LAND. BEACH. INTERCUT

The Kens continue to do "battle" with Ken Ryan Gosling singing his heart out.

This transitions into a "dream ballet" in a white space. The Kens dance in an expression of frustrated masculinity, helplessness, and feeling.

It culminates in dance-off and Ken Anthem. It's beautiful, actually. It's broken by:

>   KEN KINGSLEY
>   KEN! KEN!

We're back on the beach. The Kens hold hands post dream ballet, Ken Ryan Gosling still in the feeling, Ken Kingsley comes running over to him.

>   KEN KINGSLEY
>   KEN! Weren't we supposed to vote
>   today?

>   KEN RYAN GOSLING
>   What?

>   KEN KINGSLEY
>   To change the constitution?!

>   KEN RYAN GOSLING
>   That's today, isn't it?!

INT. BARBIE SUPREME COURT. BARBIE/KEN LAND. DAY

We move through the crowd of enthusiastic Barbies. "The last time I saw you you were brain washed! So were you! You look so much better not in the cheerleader costume! And you without the school girl outfit!"

Barbie Issa bangs the gavel, casually and glamorously commanding.

>   BARBIE ISSA
>   OK ladies, let's do this. All those
>   in favor of letting Barbie Land be
>   Barbie Land, say "Aye!"

The Barbies all say "aye" voting to retain the constitution. Sasha grabs her mom's hand. She has a tear running down her cheek.

Barbie Margot smiles. _That's_ what she wanted to show them.

EXT. BARBIE DREAMHOUSE. DAY

The Kens, in musical dance pack, approach the cul-de-sac as
if they're riding horses, but they're just galloping on foot
Monty Python style...

As they arrive, they look up and down and all around to
discover that the Barbies (plus Allan and Sasha and Gloria
and the rejected dolls) are now occupying all the houses.

The whole aesthetic is now a combination of Mojo Dojo Casa
House PLUS Dreamhouse PLUS Weirdhouse. It's a combo-pack,
which is actually the most beautiful of all.

                    KEN RYAN GOSLING
                (losing his shit)
            Is it my imagination, or are these
            Mojo Dojo Casa Houses...
            dreamier???

The Barbies all step out into the open.

                    BARBIE ISSA
                (from on high)
            That's because they're Dream
            Houses, mother*******.

She's censored by a Mattel logo.

                    BARBIE ISSA
            We've re-instated the constitution
            of Barbie Land the way it was MEANT
            to be, and returned all the
            Barbie's brains and autonomy.

All the Barbies cheer!

                    BARBIE ISSA
            And we seriously disinfected the
            houses.

                    KEN RYAN GOSLING
            Kens!!!

They all slowly, tiredly line themselves up.

                    KEN KINGSLEY
            Who are we attacking, sir?

                    KEN RYAN GOSLING
                The--

Ken Ryan Gosling looks at the Barbies, triumphant, but not
confrontational.

He hesitates. He looks back at the Kens who look exhausted and confused. Suddenly he sees the folly of everything. The other Kens look sheepish, as well. They look like the kids at the end of Lord of The Flies when the ship comes.

Ken Ryan Gosling starts crying and runs past Barbie Margot into the Dreamhouse.

> KEN RYAN GOSLING
> DON'T LOOK AT ME!!!!!

Which makes Allan cry. Barbie Margot goes into the Dreamhouse to comfort him:

Ken Ryan Gosling is lying face down on the bed.

> BARBIE MARGOT
> (to Ken Ryan Gosling)
> Hey, are you okay?

> KEN RYAN GOSLING
> (snort)
> Yeah... I'm fine. Totally.

> BARBIE MARGOT
> It's OK if you're crying. I cried
> too. It's kind of amazing.

> KEN RYAN GOSLING
> (sobbing)
> I know. I'm a liberated man. I know
> crying isn't weak.

> BARBIE MARGOT
> Do you want to sit up for a minute?

He does.

> KEN RYAN GOSLING
> (still crying)
> It was hard running stuff. I didn't
> love it.

> BARBIE MARGOT
> I get it.

> KEN RYAN GOSLING
> (crying harder)
> And those mini-fridges are so
> small! You can only fit like a six-
> pack in them, and the freezers are
> basically USELESS.
> (MORE)

                    KEN RYAN GOSLING (CONT'D)
          And, to be honest, once I found out
          patriarchy isn't about horses, I
          kind of lost interest anyway...

He heaves and ugly cries, snot dripping from his nose. Barbie
Margot tries to comfort him but kind of realizes she should
just let this finish on its own.

                    BARBIE MARGOT
          That's OK!

                    KEN RYAN GOSLING
          I always thought this would be our
          house.

                    BARBIE MARGOT
          Oh... Ken.
              (gently)
          I think I owe you an apology. I'm
          sorry I took you for granted. Not
          every night had to be girl's night.

Ken wipes his tears, nods a thank you. We see that Ken is
reflected in Barbie's eye - Ken sees it too. He leans in for
a kiss. She backs away.

                    BARBIE MARGOT
          No, I didn't mean to suggest--

                    KEN RYAN GOSLING
              (standing up)
          I don't know who I am without you!

                    BARBIE MARGOT
          You're Ken.

                    KEN RYAN GOSLING
          But it's Barbie AND Ken. There is
          no *just Ken*. That's why I was
          created - I only exist within the
          warmth of your gaze. Without you
          I'm just some blonde guy who can't
          do flips.

Ken Ryan Gosling runs to the edge of the house, dramatically.

                    BARBIE MARGOT
          Maybe it's time for you to discover
          who Ken is.

Ken leans in AGAIN for the kiss.

          BARBIE MARGOT   KEN RYAN GOSLING
No-- That's not what I'm--   OK, I think I got it.

Ken is bursting with feeling, leaning over a few more times to try to kiss her even though he knows that's not the solution. He just tries to accept it. He looks crazy.

                    KEN RYAN GOSLING
          I feel so stupid. I look SO stupid.
          I LOOK SO STUPID!!!!

                    ALL THE KENS DOWN BELOW
          NO! YOU LOOK SO COOL!!

                    BARBIE MARGOT
          Ken, you have to figure out who you
          are without me. You're not your
          girlfriend, you're not your house,
          you're not your mink.

                    KEN RYAN GOSLING
          Beach?

                    BARBIE MARGOT
          No, not even beach. Maybe all the
          things you thought made you you
          aren't... really you. Maybe it's
          Barbie AND... it's Ken.

                    KEN RYAN GOSLING
          Ken... is me?

                    BARBIE MARGOT
          YES!

                    KEN RYAN GOSLING
          Ken is me!

                    BARBIE MARGOT
               (quietly, to herself)
          And I'm Barbie...

                    KEN RYAN GOSLING
          KEN IS ME!

The Kens call out from below.

                    KEN KINGSLEY
          And ME!

                    KEN SIMU
          And ME!

Ken Ryan Gosling clutches his mink in his arms as he looks down to Ken Kingsley. And then he tosses it dramatically into the air.

                    KEN RYAN GOSLING
          I want you to have it.

Ken Kingsley dons the faux mink coat. He turns to the crowd:

                    KEN KINGSLEY
               (with all the gravitas)
          We were only fighting because we
          didn't know who we were.

Ken Ryan Gosling goes down the slide

                    KEN RYAN GOSLING
          Ken is me!!!!

Suddenly, there is clapping. And weeping. The Mattel CEO
exits the treehouse. He is somehow clapping and weeping the
hardest.

                    MATTEL CEO
               (weeping)
          Ken is RIGHT. It is SO HARD to be a
          leader.

He sees Midge standing next to him, screams.

                    MATTEL CEO
          AHHHH!!!! Midge. God. I thought we
          discontinued her.
               (recovering)
          Do you know how many times I've
          just wanted to stand up in a board
          meeting and say, "Let's just tickle
          each other!" Let's have a company
          retreat and just tickle each other!

The Mattel execs all join in and tickle their CEO, who is
giggling like a little kid. Aaron Dinkins' tickle turning
into a hug:

                    MATTEL CEO
          NO NO NO don't hug me!
               (moving on...)
          But thanks to the Barbies I too can
          relieve myself of this heavy
          existential burden while holding
          onto the very <u>real</u> title of CEO and
          we can restore everything in Barbie
          Land to exactly the way it was.

          BARBIE ISSA   MATTEL CEO
But, Mr. Mattel--   Please call me Mother.

                    BARBIE ISSA
          No thank you.
               (stepping forward)
          I don't think it should go back to
          just the way it was.
               (looking to Weird Barbie)
          No Barbie or Ken should be living
          in the shadows.

                    ALLAN
          Or Allan.

Nobody notices he says this. President Barbie approaches
Weird Barbie:

                    BARBIE ISSA
          I'm sorry we called you Weird
          Barbie behind your back and also to
          your face.

                    WEIRD BARBIE
          That's OK, I'm owning it now.

                    BARBIE ISSA
          Would you like a job in my cabinet?

                    WEIRD BARBIE
          May I please have sanitation?

                    BARBIE ISSA
          It's yours.

A gaggle of Kens approach, excited.

                    KEN KINGSLEY
          Madame President, please could the
          Kens get one Supreme Court justice?

                    BARBIE ISSA
          Whoa whoa, I can't do that. But
          maybe a lower circuit court
          judgeship--

                    KEN SIMU
          We accept! As long as we can wear
          robes.

                    HELEN MIRREN (V.O)
          Well the Kens have to start
          somewhere. And one day the Kens
          will have as much power and
          influence in Barbie Land as women
          have in the real world.

Sasha pokes at Gloria, prompting her.

> GLORIA
> (role reversal to her
> daughter)
> *Okay*, stop! I'll do it! STOP!
> (to the group, brave
> voice)
> I've got an idea.

> MATTEL CEO
> (to Gloria, making weird
> eye contact)
> Tell me your secret dream child.

> GLORIA
> (interrupting)
> What about, "Ordinary Barbie."
> (brainstorming, excited)
> She's not extraordinary! She just
> has a flattering top and wants to
> get through the day! Because it's
> OK to just want to be a mom or to
> want to be president or a mom who
> is president or not a mom who is
> also not president.

The Mattel CEO looks at Mattel Executive #1 who quickly runs
the numbers on an iPad.

> MATTEL CEO
> That's a terrible idea.

> MATTEL EXECUTIVE #1
> Yeah that's going to make money.

> MATTEL CEO
> Oh! "Ordinary Barbie." I love it.

> MATTEL CEO
> Ok! We're good, everyone good?
> (to the everyone)
> Let's now do the work to restore
> the portal between our worlds.

Everyone cheers. Sasha finds Barbie Margot in the crowd.
Barbie Margot claps, and looks happy, but something is
missing too.

> SASHA
> Hey wait, what about Barbie?

> MATTEL CEO
> What do you mean?

The Barbies nod.

                    BARBIES/KENS
          Yeah, what about Barbie?!/What's
          her ending?

                    SASHA
          What does *she* get?

                    MATTEL CEO
               (that's easy)
          Oh, that's easy! She's in love with
          Ken.

                    SASHA
          That's not her ending!

                    BARBIE MARGOT
          I'm not in love with Ken.

                    MATTEL CEO
               (flustered)
          Well what *do* you want?

                    BARBIE MARGOT
               (tears up)
          I, I don't know... I'm not really
          sure where I belong anymore. I
          don't think I have an ending.

                    A VOICE ON THE WIND
          That was always the point. I
          created you so you <u>wouldn't</u> have an
          ending.

Coming toward her on the road, backlit by the sun, is a
small, well dressed woman holding a hand bag.

                    BARBIE MARGOT
               (quietly)
          It's you.

It's Ruth, the woman from the 50's kitchen in the Mattel
offices. Barbie Margot meets her half-way:

                    BARBIE MARGOT
          You're Ruth, from Mattel.

Then Ruth goes from being some ethereal God-like figure to a
comedian, angelic act dropped.

                    RUTH
          Baby I *am* Mattel, until the IRS got
          to me, which is another movie.
                         (MORE)

                         RUTH (CONT'D)
          I Remington Steeled it for a while
          with my husband, but I'm the brains
          of the operation.

                         BARBIE MARGOT
          So you're...?

                         RUTH
               (little bow)
          Ruth Handler, inventor of Barbie.

                         MATTEL CEO
               (stage whisper)
          Her ghost keeps an office on the
          17th floor.

Whispers and looks amongst the Barbies and Kens.

                         RUTH
          What? You think the lady who
          invented Barbie looked like Barbie?
          Ha! I'm a five foot nothing Grandma
          with a double mastectomy and tax
          evasion issues. Nobody looks like
          Barbie. Except, of course, Barbie.
          Take a bow, honey.

                         BARBIE MARGOT
          I don't feel like Barbie though,
          not anymore.

Ruth gestures to Barbie Margot.

                         RUTH
          Walk with me.

Barbie takes Ruth's hand. They head down the road. The cul-de-
sac of Barbies and Kens and Mattel all do a slow theater wave
goodbye. Ken Ryan waves, heartfelt:

                         KEN RYAN GOSLING
          Thank you, Barbie. Thank you.

INT. ORIGIN SPACE

A vast empty space, almost like reflecting sand on a beach,
softly illuminated by different, changing colors.

                         RUTH
          Tell me your troubles.

                         BARBIE MARGOT
          Is this therapy?

                    RUTH
No, you're talking to a ghost from
the 1950s!

                    BARBIE MARGOT
Well, I don't know what I'm
supposed to do... I've always just
been Stereotypical Barbie, I don't
think I'm good at anything else.

                    RUTH
You saved Barbie Land from
patriarchy.

                    BARBIE MARGOT
That was very much a group effort.

                    RUTH
And you helped that Mother and
Daughter connect.

                    BARBIE MARGOT
They really helped each other.

                    RUTH
Maybe you're Self-Effacing Barbie?

                    BARBIE MARGOT
Maybe I'm not Barbie anymore.

Barbie Margot says this before she realized that she'd said
it and then immediately realizes it's true.

                    RUTH
You understand that humans only
have *one* ending. Ideas live
forever, humans, not so much. You
know that right?

                    BARBIE MARGOT
I do.

                    RUTH
Being a human can be pretty
uncomfortable.

                    BARBIE MARGOT
I know.

                    RUTH
I mean humans make things up like
patriarchy and Barbie just to deal
with how uncomfortable it is.

                    BARBIE MARGOT
          I understand.

                    RUTH
          And then you die.

                    BARBIE MARGOT
               (nodding)
          I want... I want to be part of the
          people that make meaning, not the
          thing that's made. I want to be the
          one imagining, not the idea itself.
          Does that make sense?

                    RUTH
               (chuckling)
          I always knew that Barbie would
          surprise me, but I never expected
          this.

                    BARBIE MARGOT
          Do you give me permission? To
          become human?

                    RUTH
          You don't need _my_ permission.

                    BARBIE MARGOT
          But you're The Creator. You control
          me.

                    RUTH
          Ha! I can't control you any more
          than I could control my own
          daughter! I named you after her -
          Barbara. And I always hoped for you
          like I hoped for her. We mothers
          stand still so our daughters can
          look back to see how far they've
          come.

                    BARBIE MARGOT
               (figuring it out)
          So being human isn't something I
          need to ask for or even want, it's
          something I discover I am...?

                    RUTH
          I can't, in good conscience, let
          you take that leap without knowing
          what it means. Take my hands.

She does.

                    RUTH
          Now close your eyes.

She does.

                    RUTH
          Now... FEEL.

We see details of Barbie Margot, her eye, her forearm, her
pulse. Life.

And she feels and sees what a human life is. The joy and pain
of being mortal. All that she will lose and gain.

We see FLASHES of life lived, unadorned home footage of many
women's lives - happiness, sadness, big moments, little
moments, childhood, adulthood, old age, how it all rushes by
in one moment, each life drifting into the next somehow
capturing the current that runs through all things.

BACK TO BARBIE: Tears roll down Barbie Margot's face. She
opens her eyes and says one thing:

                    BARBIE MARGOT
          YES.

EXT. REAL WORLD. LOS ANGELES. DAY

We BOOM down to the streets of LA.

                    HELEN MIRREN (V.O.)
          So Barbie left behind the pastels
          and plastic of Barbie Land for the
          pastels and plastic of Los Angeles.

Gloria pulls up to the curb. Nerdy Well Meaning Dad rides
shotgun, Sasha and Barbie Margot in the backseat.

                    BARBIE MARGOT
               (excited, anxious)
          Well, thanks for the lift.

          GLORIA   SASHA
You've got this.   I'm so proud of you.

                    NERDY WELL MEANING DAD
          Estoy muy orgullosa de ti.

                    BARBIE MARGOT
          Thank you, you guys are the best.
          Ok, lets do this.

                    NERDY WELL MEANING DAD
          Sí se puede!

                         GLORIA
            That's a political statement.

                         SASHA
            That's appropriation, Dad!

They all cheer her on as she walks from the car into a big
building. We see that she's wearing Birkenstocks - PINK, of
course, but still, Birks.

INT. OFFICE. CONTINUOUS.

Nervous, happy, she finds the right door, and walks up to a
reception desk. To the woman behind the glass:

                    BARBIE MARGOT
            Hi...

                    RECEPTIONIST
            Name?

                    BARBIE MARGOT
            Oh, um, Handler comma Barbara.

                    RECEPTIONIST
            And what are you here for today,
            Barbara?

And then she says, with so much pride, so much anticipation,
so much meaning, so much deep joy:

                    BARBIE MARGOT
            I'm here to see my gynecologist.

CUT TO BLACK BEFORE ANYONE CAN EVEN PROCESS THAT SENTENCE.

The End.

BARBIE

Gallery of Images